RETAILING CAREER STARTER

by Valerie Lipow

LEARNINGEXPRESS

LearningExpress ♦ New York

Library of Congress Cataloging-in-Publication Data

Lipow, Valerie.
  Retailing career starter/by Valerie Lipow.
     p.   cm.—(Career starters)
  ISBN 1-57685-149-4
  1. Retail trade—Vocational guidance—United States. 2. Selling—States. I. Title.
II. Series.
HF5429.3.L57   1998
381'.1'02373—dc21   98-37939
                                                              CIP

Printed in the United States of America
9 8 7 6 5 4 3 2 1
First Edition

Regarding the Information in this Book

Every effort has been made to ensure accuracy of directory information up until press time. However, phone numbers and/or addresses are subject to change. Please contact the respective organization for the most recent information.

For Further Information

For information on LearningExpress, other LearningExpress products, or bulk sales, please call or write to us at:

LearningExpress®
900 Broadway
Suite 604
New York, NY 10003
212-995-2566

LearningExpress is an affiliated company of Random House, Inc.

ISBN 1-57685-149-4

7 85555 85149 8

CONTENTS

INTRODUCTION

WHY ENTER THE RETAIL SALES FIELD?

People want to buy products and services to help them look better, feel better, and have better lives. Retailers provide the vehicle for these products and services. Consumer spending through retail stores accounts for two-thirds of U.S. economic activity. One out of five workers in the United States is employed by the retail industry. The majority of retail employees work directly with customers on the selling floor or in a sales-related position.

With over one million retail establishments in the United States, the retail industry currently employs over 20 million workers. Every year, vast numbers of entry-level jobs in retail are created. Since the beginning of the 1990s, the retail sector has created 700,000 jobs, representing 13% of all new jobs in the U.S. According to the U.S. Department of Labor, more than 15% of all new jobs created in the next seven years will be in retailing. Retail employment is expected to increase to 24 million workers by the year 2005. Projected growth in retail employment is 300% greater than that of manufacturing.

With so many jobs, breaking into retail sales is easy for anyone who enjoys people and is willing to work hard. This book tells you about the hottest entry-level positions in retailing and how you can land great jobs in these areas.

Even if you've never gone to college, you can get your retail career going quickly if you're a high-energy person. Most retail sales jobs can be obtained without a four-year college degree, although people who have a college education have a wider range of opportunities in this fast-growing field, and usually can get into management jobs faster. The training required to become a retail sales associate varies; it can be on-the-job training (OJT), certificate programs that can be completed within a few months, two-year associate degree programs, or four-year bachelor's degree programs.

In chapter one, you'll get an inside look at the hottest retail jobs. You'll find out what retail sales associates do, see specific job descriptions, typical salaries, advancement opportunities, hiring trends, and the skills and abilities needed. You'll learn about types of work settings and their typical hiring procedures. Finally, there's a step-by-step checklist for entering and succeeding in this growing industry.

Chapter two tells you how formal training will help you get a jump start on your career in retail, and you'll learn how to select and evaluate training programs near you. You'll find sample courses that are taught in actual retail training programs for each of the hottest entry-level job titles in this book. These course descriptions can help you decide what occupation is right for you and how long you need to go to school for each one. To help you evaluate the quality of different training programs, use the checklist in chapter two to prepare tough questions to ask the admissions counselors in training programs you're considering. Then you'll find tips on how to make the most out of your training program, such as studying for exams, taking great notes in class, and networking with other students.

In chapter three, you'll find a review of the different types of training programs available to you. There's information on the common majors offered by technical schools, colleges, and universities that will lay the groundwork for your career in retailing. You'll see several sample course descriptions that will give you an idea of what material is covered and how many classroom hours are required. You'll also discover a directory of retail sales training programs that will provide you with a representative listing of schools across the country. This can help you if you're considering moving away from your home town. So that you can contact each school directly to get more information and request application forms, all listings include the school name, address, and phone and/or fax number.

Chapter four offers up-to-date information about how financial aid programs can help you pay for the training program that's right for you. A step-by-step look at the financial aid process will help you to prepare all the information you need so you can complete the application forms and have the best chance at getting the aid you need.

Chapter five shows you how to land the job you want once you've completed your training program. You'll find hot leads on where to look for job openings and the latest tips on networking, writing resumes and cover letters, and using the World Wide Web to find your dream job.

Finally, chapter six shows you what you need to know to succeed once you've landed your job.

Once you've got your foot in the retail door, anything you might want to do in the business world, from advertising to buying to management and more, is there. So read on to find out how you can enter and succeed in the exciting and growing retailing industry!

CHAPTER | 1

This chapter describes the hottest entry-level retail sales jobs you can get with two years of training or less, so you can begin your career as soon as possible. It includes specific job descriptions, typical salaries, advancement opportunities, hiring trends, and the skills needed for each job. You'll learn about the steps it takes to become a retail sales associate.

THE HOTTEST RETAIL SALES JOBS AND HOW TO GET THEM

Retail sales professionals work in every city and town, from little stores on Main Street to giant department stores to specialized stores in every mall. Sales associates work with customers who shop in the store as well as with managers, buyers, and other employees within the organization.

The job descriptions in this chapter will show you what's involved in being a retail sales associate and how to match up your abilities and interests to each of them. You'll also find out why retailing is an exciting industry, as well as what types of advancement opportunities are available.

WHY BECOME A RETAIL SALES ASSOCIATE?

There are three excellent reasons to consider a career in retailing: money, opportunity for advancement, and the ability to enter the industry with varying amounts of training. Let's look at these now.

Money

Put aside your stereotypes about minimum wage as the pinnacle for earnings in retailing. Store managers can make some serious money, some earning up to six figures. Although there are plenty of jobs paying minimum wage, you can make great money in retail, working either in or out of store operations. Keep reading this chapter for facts on retailing opportunities outside of store operations.

According to the International Mass Retail Association, starting salaries in retailing are on par with what are traditionally perceived as high-paying jobs in business (such as banking, accounting, and communications). For example, an average entry-level annual salary in retail for a buyer or merchandiser is $27,959 as compared to an average entry-level salary in banking of $29,917.

Here are some sample entry-level salaries in retail:

Logistics/Distribution:	$23,714/year
Buying/Merchandising:	$26,120/year
Information Systems:	$30,957/year
Finance:	$24,143/year
Store Operations:	$26,757/year

You could be earning up to $122,000 a year in store operations or over $80,000 a year in merchandising in less time than you might think. The U. S. Department of Labor says that a commission sales professional with a healthy client list can earn more than $100,000 per year!

Exploding Job Growth

The retail sales industry is growing every year. This growth fuels the need for enthusiastic and flexible sales clerks, cashiers, and management trainees. The Bureau of Labor Statistics of the United States Department of Labor shows that the retail industry will continue to expand significantly in the future.

The demand for entry-level retail personnel is due not only to growth in the number of retail stores, but because there is high turnover as people leave the field or get promoted to more responsible, higher paying jobs.

"Almost everything we have or use is sold by someone," reminds Ron S. La Vine, a telemarketing sales trainer in Oak Park, California. "The big advantage is there is always work for a good salesperson who is attentive, polite, courteous, respectful, and willing to go the extra step to make the customer happy. The key to entering retail sales is to find quality products and services you feel good about selling. It is very important you believe what you have to offer is of benefit to the consumer."

Retail sales workers need to be flexible and creative to advance in the job market. Experts advise that successful retail employees of the future will be those who are committed to continuous improvement to keep up with technological changes and competition, and with the changes in the industry's future.

Minimum level of training

You can become a retail sales associate without a college degree, which is why these jobs attract people who need to find a job without a lot of training. Many employers offer training on the job.

Still, almost every company requires entry-level employees to have a high school diploma or GED (high school equivalency certificate) as a minimum education requirement. Why? Because the diploma or GED demonstrates the person has adequate reading, writing, and math skills, and they show the employer that you have the potential to learn and increase your skill level and become a more valuable employee in the future.

If you're in high school now, attend classes regularly, study hard, and graduate. Take courses that make you think critically, solve problems and communicate with others; these include English, math, speech, history, and science. Take computer and business courses if they are available. Participate in athletics, student government, or clubs to develop your leadership, teamwork, and communication skills.

If you left school without a high school diploma, you can earn a GED through your local adult education center or community college. GED preparation

---

Listen to this common complaint from retail sales managers:

"We have spent weeks—*months*—interviewing prospective salespeople and no one seems to care about the job. There is this unbelievable lack of interest, although these jobs offer good opportunity and an attractive benefit package. People tend to look at jobs in sales as 'just another job' rather than a career."

You can see there's a tremendous demand for motivated and qualified retail employees. If you want a career—and not just a "job"—in this industry, they're out there!

classes are offered if you need them; or, you can take the standardized GED test without any class work.

ENTRY-LEVEL RETAIL JOBS
Entry-Level Jobs Available Without Training

The most common entry-level retail positions are sales clerk, counter or rental clerk, and cashier. They may also be known by other job titles, such as sales associate, or customer service clerk. Many of these jobs are available without specialized training; many people learn these positions in on-the-job training and experience.

Although these jobs may seem to be at the lower end of retail careers, they offer you a chance to get a feel for retailing and to compare your own interests and qualifications with the requirements of the business.

Below are more details about these positions.

SALES ASSOCIATES

$10/Hour through training. What's in a name? In our case, super-aggressive men and women who want to take on an organization like ours and redefine it. Our name may be Levitz, but our personality is all yours. Interested? We're building a high performance, customer-driven sales team in one of the area's most beautiful home furnishing stores. You'll also need great communication skills and high expectations. We will provide the training and the environment in which you can achieve your goals. If you have what we need, we want to talk to you. Please apply in person at our Tukwila store located at 17601 S. Center Pkwy or fax your resume to (206) 575-8112. EOE Levitz

---

Retail Sales Clerk

Job Description: Whether selling clothing, books, pets, audio CDs, or power tools, retail sales clerks help customers find what they are looking for and try to entice them to buy. They may describe the item's features or benefits, demonstrating its use, or showing various models, sizes, or colors. For some positions, particularly those selling expensive or complex items such as diamond jewelry, cars, or computers, the clerk may need special knowledge or skills.

Most retail clerks, especially those who work in department and apparel stores, make out sales checks; receive cash, check, and charge account payments; bag or package purchases; and give change and receipts. Depending on the hours they work, they may have to open or close cash registers. This may include counting the money; separating charge slips, coupons, and exchange vouchers; and making deposits at the cash office. They may also handle returns and exchanges of merchandise, and wrap gifts. In addition, they may help stock shelves or racks, arrange for mailing or delivery of purchases, mark price tags, take inventory, and prepare displays. They may also be responsible for keeping their work areas neat.

Typical Salaries: The starting wage for many retail sales positions is the federal minimum wage. In some areas where employers are having difficulty attracting and retaining workers, wages are higher than the established minimum.

Sales clerks in 1996 earned a median income between $265 and $593 per week. Workers who sold high-ticket items (boats, home entertainment systems, and home furnishings) earned more on average than those who sold less expensive items (hardware and building supplies, clothing and accessories).

Keep in mind that in retailing, depending on the kind of business, some salespeople are paid an hourly wage, some by commission (earning a percentage of the sales they make), or a combination of wages and commissions. Under a commission system, the employee has the opportunity to significantly increase their earnings above the hourly wage, but they may find their earnings depend on their ability to sell their product. These earnings may vary significantly over time, depending on the ups and downs of the economy. Employers may use incentive programs such as awards, banquets, and profit-sharing plans to motivate and promote teamwork among the sales staff.

Hiring Trends: According to the U.S. Department of Labor's statistics, sales clerks held over 4.5 million jobs in 1996. The largest employers are department stores, clothing and accessories stores, furniture and home furnishing stores, and motor vehicle dealers. Jobs are plentiful and are available in every area of the country.

Personal Abilities and Personality Traits Needed: The ability to provide courteous and efficient service, using tact and patience, is crucial for sales clerks who want to get ahead in retail. Stamina, flexibility, and the ability to keep your energy high under stress or long hours in also important. Good English and math skills, as well as a good memory, are needed too.

Advancement Opportunities: With experience, sales clerks usually move up to positions of greater responsibility and may be given their choice of departments. This often means moving to areas with potentially higher earnings and commissions. The highest earnings potential is usually found in selling big-ticket items, such as cars and home furnishings. This type of position often requires the most knowledge of the product and the greatest selling ability.

Today, large retail businesses generally prefer to hire college graduates as management trainees, making a college education increasingly important. Despite this trend, capable employees without college degrees should still be able to advance to administrative or supervisory positions in large establishments.

Opportunities for advancement vary in small stores. In some establishments, advancement is limited, because one person, often the owner, does most of the managerial work. In others, however, some sales workers are promoted to assistant managers.

Retail selling experience may be an asset when applying for sales positions with larger retailers or in other industries, such as financial services, wholesale trade, or manufacturing.

A variety of jobs are available for people with some retail sales experience without getting a specialized business education. All of these people use sales techniques, along with their knowledge of merchandise, to assist customers and encourage purchases. These include:

Customer service representative

Sales representative

Real estate sales agent

Insurance agent

Bank teller

Postal service clerk

Check the **Occupational Outlook Handbook** in your local library or on the World Wide Web at [insert web address] for more information about these occupations.

Retail Cashier

Job Description: Supermarkets, department stores, gasoline service stations, movie theaters, restaurants, and many other businesses employ cashiers to register the sale of their merchandise. Cashiers total bills, receive money, make change, fill out charge forms, and give receipts. Cashiers must know the store's policies and procedures for accepting each type of payment the store accepts. For checks and charges, they may have to request additional identification from the customer or get authorization from a supervisor or other source. When the sale is complete, cashiers issue a receipt to the customer and return the appropriate change. They may also wrap or bag the purchase.

As a cashier, you will count the contents of your cash register or cash drawer at the beginning and end of your shifts. You'll usually separate charge forms, return slips, coupons, and any other non-cash items. You'll also handle returns and exchanges and ensure that merchandise is in good condition and determine where, when, and how it was purchased.

Depending on the type of establishment, you may have other duties as well. In many supermarkets, for example, cashiers weigh produce and bulk food as well as return unwanted items to the shelves. In convenience stores, cashiers may be required to know how to use a variety of machines other than cash registers, and how to furnish money orders. Operating ticket-dispensing machines and answering customers' questions are common duties for cashiers who work at movie theaters and ticket agencies.

Typical Salaries: Cashiers have earnings ranging from the minimum wage to several times that amount. Wages tend to be higher in areas where there is intense competition for workers.

According to the Bureau of Labor Statistics, in 1996, median weekly earnings for full-time cashiers were $247. The middle 50 percent earned between $198 and $328; 10 percent earned below $165; and 10 percent earned above $486.

Hiring Trends: The Department of Labor notes that cashiers held about 3,146,000 jobs in 1996. Although employed in nearly every industry, nearly one-third of all cashiers worked in supermarkets and other food stores. Department stores, gasoline service stations, drug stores, and other retail establishments also employed large numbers of cashiers. Job opportunities are found throughout the country.

Cashier employment is expected to increase about as fast as the average for all occupations through the year 2006 due to expanding demand for goods and services by a growing population.

Personal Abilities and Personality Traits Needed: If you work as a cashier, you'll need to perform repetitious work accurately. You'll also need basic arithmetic skills and good manual dexterity; and, because cashiers deal constantly with the public, you must be neat in appearance and able to deal tactfully and pleasantly with customers. In addition, some firms seek persons who have operated specialized equipment or who have business experience, such as typing, selling, or handling money.

Advancement Opportunities: Advancement opportunities for cashiers vary. For those working part-time, promotion may be to a full-time position. Others advance to head cashier or cash office clerk. In addition, this job offers a good opportunity to learn a particular business and can serve as a stepping stone to more responsible positions.

Counter/Rental Clerk

Job Description: Whether renting videotapes or automobiles, dropping off clothes to be dry-cleaned or appliances to be serviced, counter and rental clerks answer questions involving product availability, cost, and rental agreements. Counter and rental clerks also take orders, calculate fees, receive payments, and accept returns.

Regardless of where you work as a counter or rental clerk you must be knowledgeable about the company's products, services, policies, and procedures. Depending on the type of establishment, counter and rental clerks use their special knowledge to give advice on a variety of products and services. For example, in the car rental industry, they inform customers about the features of the different types of vehicles available and daily and weekly rental costs, ensure that customers meet age and other requirements, and indicate when and in what condition cars must be returned. In repair or dry-cleaning establishments, counter clerks inform customers when items will be ready.

When taking orders, counter and rental clerks use various types of equipment. In some establishments, they write out tickets and order forms. However, computers and bar code scanners are quickly becoming the norm. Most of these computer systems are user friendly and usually require very little data entry.

Typical Salaries: Counter and rental clerks typically start at the federal minimum wage. In areas where there is intense competition for workers, however, wages are often higher. In addition to wages, some counter and rental clerks receive commissions, based on the number of contracts they complete or services they sell.

Retail counter clerks earned a median weekly income of $303 in 1996. The middle 50 percent earned between $230 and $489 a week. The bottom 10 percent earned less than $184; the top 10 percent earned more than $631.

Hiring Trends: Counter and rental clerks held 374,000 jobs in 1996. About 25 percent worked for videotape rental establishments. Other large employers included laundries or dry cleaners, automobile rental firms, equipment rental firms, and miscellaneous entertainment and recreation establishments.

Counter and rental clerks are employed throughout the country but are concentrated in metropolitan areas, where personal services and renting and leasing services are in greater demand.

Employment for rental and counter clerks is expected to increase faster than the average for all occupations through the year 2006, due to anticipated employment growth in the industries where they are concentrated—business services, automotive rentals, and amusement and recreation services.

Personal Abilities and Personality Traits Needed: Counter and rental clerks should enjoy working with people and have the ability to deal tactfully with difficult customers. In addition, good oral and written communication skills are essential.

Advancement Opportunities: These will depend on the size and type of company. Many establishments that employ counter or rental clerks tend to be small businesses. This makes advancing difficult. But in larger establishments with a corporate structure, jobs as counter and rental clerks offer good opportunities for employees to learn about the company's products and business practices. These jobs can be stepping stones to more responsible positions, because it's common in many stores to promote counter and rental clerks into assistant manager positions.

ON-THE JOB TRAINING FOR ENTRY-LEVEL RETAIL POSITIONS

Nearly all entry-level sales clerks, cashiers, and rental/counter clerks are trained on the job. In small firms, experienced workers often train beginners. The first day is usually spent observing the operation and becoming familiar with the store's equipment, policies, and procedures. After this, trainees are assigned to a register—frequently under the supervision of a more experienced worker.

In larger firms, before being placed at cash registers, trainees can spend anywhere from several hours to up to a few weeks in formal classroom training. Topics typically covered include a description of the industry and the company, instruction on the store's history, philosophy, policies, procedures, equipment operation, sales techniques, customer service, loss prevention, and security. Some companies use computer-based training, videotapes, brochures, and pamphlets in addition to or instead of classroom training to orient new employees.

CAN I GET EMPLOYEE BENEFITS AS AN ENTRY-LEVEL RETAIL EMPLOYEE?

Yes. Benefits for full-time sales associates, counter clerks, or cashiers tend to be better than for those working part time. Full-time employees often receive health and life insurance and paid vacations. In addition, many often receive discounts on purchases, and cashiers in restaurants may receive free or low-cost meals. Some employers also offer employee stock option plans.

WHAT ABOUT TEMPORARY OR PART-TIME JOBS?

This is where retail has it head and shoulders above most other industries: for earning while you are learning, and discovering whether working in this environment is for you!

Opportunities for summer, holiday, or part-time employment for sales clerks, rental and counter clerks, and cashiers are plentiful. In 1994, almost seven million retail employees (nearly one-third of all retail employees) were part-time workers. Many students rely on retail employment. A part-time or temporary job in retail is an important and flexible way to earn money while pursuing an education, and is a wonderful way to evaluate whether a career in this field is for you. In 1993, almost 17% of all retail employees were enrolled in school—1.5 million were in high school, and almost 1.8 million were working their way through college.

Working behind the counter or on the sales floor gives you first-hand contact with customers; during holidays, sales, and other busy times you'll see how you measure up handling pressure. These temporary or part-time jobs also allow you to observe stock handling procedures (how merchandise is ordered, stored, and displayed), keep inventory records, operate a cash register or point-of-sale (POS) terminal, write up sales, handle returns and exchanges and arrange the merchandise. This experience lets you build valuable customer-service skills that are useful in many careers.

Tom Russell, President of ESC2000, a retail executive search firm in York, Pennsylvania, recalls:

> "I began my retail career while in high school as a stocker. I worked part time and then full time during summer. When I started college, I was promoted to a management trainee and continued to work part time while going to school. To me, retailing is one of the few industries where you get a chance to be 'in charge' or responsible almost immediately. Even as a management trainee, it won't be long until you are carrying keys to the store and helping to open and close. In most careers, you might spend several years at a lower-level desk job before you get to be a true manager. In retailing, it begins the first night that your Store Manager lets you close alone. That's a great feeling for a young person who wants to grow as a manager."

Entry-Level Jobs Available With Training

The retail "Management Trainee" position is the "foot in the door" available throughout the retail industry for anyone eager to climb the corporate ladder. Companies prefer to hire applicants who are familiar with the merchandise they sell as well as with retailing practices. Many companies prefer to hire college graduates for management trainee positions. Most employers use a combination of methods.

Candidates who are accepted in a retail management-training program are exposed to all aspects of the business, including brief training in merchandising, finance, marketing, operations, and human resources.

After completing the training program, trainees are selected for placement in a department where they excelled. Promotion from the management training position generally occurs after nine months to two years on the job.

Management trainees who do well may get jobs as a department manager, assistant manager, or assistant buyer. Read on to learn more about what they do.

Department/Sales Manager

Department/Sales Manager positions are the first customer contact jobs for management trainees as they develop experience and responsibility. This position includes supervision of the sales force as well as control over the sales floor inventory of merchandise. Promotion from this position typically occurs in one to two years.

Department managers are responsible for ensuring that customers receive good service and quality goods. They also answer customers' inquiries and handle complaints. They are often responsible for interviewing, hiring, and training employees. They must prepare work schedules and assign workers to specific duties. They establish and implement policies, goals, objectives, and procedures for their specific departments; they also coordinate activities with other department heads. In general, they strive for smooth operations within their departments. They supervise employees who price and ticket goods and place them on display; clean and organize shelves, displays, and inventory in stockrooms; and inspect merchandise to ensure that none is outdated. Supervisors and managers increasingly must be computer literate since cash registers and inventory control systems have become computerized. Department managers review inventory and sales records, develop merchandising techniques, coordinate sales promotions, and may greet and assist customers to promote sales and good public relations.

In small or independent retail stores, supervisors not only directly supervise sales associates, but are also responsible for the operation of the entire store. In these instances, they may be called store managers. Some are also store owners.

Most retail supervisors work at least 40 hours a week, and often more. They may work many more hours during holidays, busy shopping hours and seasons, sales, and when inventory is taken. They are expected to work evenings and weekends but usually are compensated by getting a weekday off. Hours can change weekly, and managers sometimes must report to work on short notice, especially when employees are absent.

According to the U.S. Department of Labor, retail sales supervisors and managers held about 929,000 wage and salary jobs in 1996. This doesn't include the thousands who own and operate their own stores. Most department managers work in grocery, department, and clothing and accessory stores.

The Labor Department points out that the number of jobs in retail management will be relatively slow through 2006, because retail companies prefer to hire more sales staff and fewer supervisors and managers. However, many job openings are expected to occur as experienced supervisors and managers move into higher levels of management, change jobs from one company to another, go on to other careers, or leave the labor force.

The Retail Manager

The responsibilities of retail supervisors and managers vary, depending on the size and type of establishment, as well as what level of management they hold. In larger stores, supervisors specialize in one department or one aspect of merchandising. Larger organizations tend to have many layers of management. As in other industries, supervisory-level retail managers usually report to their mid-level counterparts who, in turn, report to top-level managers. Small stores, and stores that carry specialized merchandise, typically have fewer management levels.

Assistant Buyer

This is another possible career path for the management trainee position. Also known as a junior buyer or an assistant merchandise manager, this employee performs the detail functions for retail buyers and gains hands-on experience in merchandise selection, order writing, receiving, delivery, and follow-up.

Computers are having a major effect on the jobs of buyers and assistant buyers. Computers are used to obtain up-to-date product and price listings, to track inventory levels, process routine orders, and help determine when to make purchases. Computers also maintain supplier lists, record the history of supplier performance and consumer buying habits, and issue purchase orders.

Because the procurement process is becoming more automated, it is extremely important for assistant buyers to be computer literate, including knowing how to use word processing and spreadsheet software. Other important qualities include the ability to analyze technical data in suppliers' proposals, and perform financial analyses. They also need good communication, negotiation, and math skills,

Most assistant buyers work in offices within the stores, at the company's corporate headquarters, or at the service facilities. They frequently work more than a 40-hour week because of special sales, conferences, or production deadlines. Evening and weekend work is common. This is especially true before holiday seasons. Consequently, many retail firms discourage using vacation time from late November until early January.

Assistant buyers often work under pressure because retail stores are so competitive; buyers need physical stamina to keep up with the fast-paced nature of their work.

Persons who wish to be promoted from assistant buyers to buyers should be good at planning and decision making and have an interest in merchandising. Anticipating consumer preferences and ensuring that goods are in stock when they are needed require resourcefulness, good judgment, and self-confidence. Buyers must be able to make decisions quickly and take risks. Marketing skills and the ability to identify products that will sell are also very important. Employers often look for leadership ability because buyers spend a large portion of their time supervising assistant buyers and dealing with manufacturers' representatives and store executives.

Promotion from this position typically occurs in one to two years. Assistant buyers can work their way up the ranks to buyer, divisional merchandise manager, and on to senior management.

The buyer, also called a "merchandise manager," is responsible for planning sales, selecting merchandise, and writing and pricing orders. Other important responsibilities are inventory and receipts.

Buyers largely determine which products their establishment will sell. Therefore, they must be able to accurately predict what will appeal to the store's consumers. They must constantly stay informed of the latest trends; if they don't, profits would fall, and the store's reputation will suffer. Buyers also follow ads in newspapers, on television and radio (and on the Internet) to check on competitors and watch general economic conditions to anticipate consumer buying patterns.

Buyers working for large and medium-sized firms usually specialize in acquiring one or two lines of merchandise (for example, ladies' sportswear), whereas buyers working for small stores may purchase their complete inventory.

Many buyers assist in planning and implementing sales promotion programs. Working with store managers and marketing executives, they determine what kind of sale to schedule, and then purchase products accordingly. They also work with advertising personnel to create the ad campaign. For example, they may determine the media in which the advertisement will be placed—newspapers, direct mail, television, radio, the Net, or some combination thereof. In addition, they often visit the selling floor to ensure that the goods are properly displayed.

Many buyers spend at least several days a month traveling. Buyers for worldwide and large retailers, and buyers of high-fashion apparel, may travel outside the United States.

The Divisional Merchandise Manager (DMM) is responsible for a number of merchandise departments and the respective buyers. The DMM works to ensure that the team provides consistent quality and value for their customers. A major responsibility of this position is to maintain a strategic level of merchandise that supports the image of the retailer. Vendor relations, market visits, job enhancement, and education for the buying team are also important. Eight to ten years of related retail merchandising experience is typically required to become a divisional merchandise manager.

Getting a bachelor's degree in business gives you the best chance of obtaining a retail buyer job. Job growth is slow, although jobs are plentiful, because mergers and acquisitions have forced the consolidation of buying departments, thus eliminating some jobs. In addition, larger retail stores are removing their buying departments from distinct geographic areas and centralizing them at their headquarters, thereby eliminating more jobs.

WHAT OTHER RETAIL JOBS ARE THERE?

Not all retail jobs are in retail stores. In fact, 20% of retail jobs are outside of store operations. Retail isn't just about sales associates, merchandise buyers, and store managers. Retail companies are just like companies in any other industry. They have headquarters and regional offices that employ a variety of professionals in:

- Operations Management
- Promotions, Advertising, and Marketing
- Information Systems
- Loss Prevention

- Store Planning and Design
- Human Resources
- Finance

Let's review these areas now.

Operations Management

Operations or "logistics" personnel are responsible for operating and maintaining the store's physical plant, for providing various customer services, for the receipt, ticketing, warehousing, and distribution of a store's inventory, and for buying and maintaining store supplies and operating equipment.

Many excellent opportunities exist in this area for people who are more interested in retail operating activities than in retail merchandising. Some of these opportunities include vice president, store superintendent, warehouse manager, maintenance supervisor, customer service manager, receiving supervisor, and security.

Keith Koenig, Vice President and Controller for City Furniture, a multimillion dollar, 11-store company headquartered in Ft. Lauderdale, Florida, says, "I would highly encourage someone who wanted to make a high income to consider the operational and logistical side of retailing."

Promotions, Advertising, and Marketing

There is more to sales promotion than the ads you see on TV and in magazines and newspapers.

The creative departments in retail sales promotion try to persuade the customer that they need and want what the store has to sell. This approach is based on the theory that the best way to generate sales is to encourage people to want new merchandise. According to the International Mass Retail Association, retail creative departments need people to "stay ahead of the game." These people investigate the needs, wants, and buying trends of the consumer, in order to anticipate what kinds of things consumers will buy (and how much they will pay for them), and then stimulate the targeted consumer to buy from their store.

There are many aspects of sales promotions, with public relations, advertising, visual merchandising, and special events coordination being the fundamental components.

Information Systems

Widely recognized as one of the fastest growing fields in the world, computer information systems apply to a broad range of areas in the retail industry. Experience in efficient computer applications such as data capture and application, quick response (QR) inventory systems to minimize inventory cost, expedient point-of-sale (POS) systems, and electronic data interchange (EDI) ensure retailers a more efficient merchandise flow.

According to Erik Gordon, Director of the Center for Retailing Education and Research at the Warrington College of Business Administration, University of Florida, "[One of] the more exciting uses of information by retailers [is] data mining to support efficient and effective merchandise assortments and to support loyalty programs and relationship marketing."

What is "data mining?" It's how retail professionals are using computers—including computers built into point-of-sale tools such as cash registers and bar-code scanners—to gather and analyze the vast amount of information about customers and what they buy. They use the information to understand their customers, such as their ages, sex, and purchasing habits; to use, buy, and stock the kinds of retail products they know their customers are looking for; and to develop specialized advertising and marketing strategies to attract these customers to shop in their stores.

Information systems professionals are also needed to administer computer networks, complex personnel and product database systems, and Internet and Intranet sites.

In fact, just about every aspect of the retail industry involves some amount of computer use. The retail professional who possesses basic computer knowledge, as well as expertise in one or more areas, will be well prepared for a successful career in retailing.

Loss Prevention

The Loss Prevention (LP) team is an essential component to the retail industry. It is a specialized part of law enforcement and security.

LP associates have many responsibilities, and they must be multi-talented. They work to control inventory shrinkage (through shoplifting and other means), ensure employee and customer safety, and be the first to respond to emergency incidents. LP associates must be computer literate in order to analyze data and to develop methods and technologies to prevent violations and thefts. LP specialists also serve as educators, informing managers about proven practices that will ensure safety and good business.

Store Planning and Design

The design, location, and layout of a store play an enormous role in its success. Elements as subtle as lighting, aisle width, and color coordination may play a significant role in the appeal of a retail establishment to its customers.

Store planning and design associates conduct the research necessary to determine the best location, layout, and design of a store, while being open and receptive to the needs and preferences of the customer. Talented, creative people with training and education in business, architecture, art, and related fields have innumerable opportunities in this field.

Human Resources

Human Resources (HR) professionals develop, implement, and maintain human resource policies and programs. These include organizational planning and development, recruiting and hiring, employee training and development, employee relations, compensation, benefits, safety, payroll, and other employee services. The HR staff also ensures consistency of policies and practices in support of the company's goals and objectives. The HR team is also responsible for ensuring compliance to all federal and state labor laws.

Finance

In general, retail competition is fierce. Many retailers have been involved in complicated corporate restructuring efforts, involving mergers, acquisitions, and "downsizing." Most retailers operate on a tight profit margin. With such a fine line between success and failure, retailers continue to need top financial experts—and compensate them generously.

Finance professionals prepare the financial reports for all aspects of the business, including long-range forecasting and planning, economic trend analysis and budgeting, shortage control and internal audit, gross and net profit, accounts payable to vendors, and accounts receivable from charge customers.

ADVANCEMENT IN RETAIL

According to a recent survey reported by the International Mass Retail Association, the average time before a promotion in retail is one year. In retail, unlike other industries, promotion is based on performance. So, if you're smart, motivated, and hard working, there's a place for you in retail.

DO YOU HAVE WHAT IT TAKES TO BECOME A RETAIL SALES ASSOCIATE?

Retail sales associates must be creative, think logically, and have excellent communication and problem-solving skills. Take this brief quiz to see if a career in retail sales is right for you.

Is a Career In Retail Right for You?	Yes	No
Do you care about what's hot or popular in clothing or other products and services that people buy?	___	___
Do you enjoy shopping or spending time in stores?	___	___

If yes, what kinds of products or services do you most enjoy shopping for and using?

_____

_____

	Yes	No
Do you enjoy approaching people and offering to help them?	___	___
Do you enjoy talking to people?	___	___
Do you enjoy helping people find things?	___	___
Do you enjoy reading and learning about things to stay current on what's hot or popular?	___	___
Are you good at persuading people to see things the way you do?	___	___
Can you handle stress?	___	___
Are you willing to work nights or weekends when asked?	___	___

If you answered "yes" to several of these questions, chances are you would enjoy working in retail sales. Take a look at the things you listed as being products or services you enjoy shopping for; this will help you decide what kind of sales environment you'd most enjoy working in.

Someone who will be successful in retailing has a competitive personality with a broad range of abilities and characteristics. Experts say the ideal retail job-seeker should possess the following qualities:

- ◆ **"People Person":** Someone who is able to develop an understanding of the customer's wants and needs, enjoys working with people and has the tact and patience to deal with difficult customers, excels at serving them well and enthusiastically, and is a team player who gets along well with fellow employees.

- **Honesty:** Sales workers are often held responsible for the contents of their cash registers, and repeated shortages are cause for dismissal in many organizations.

- **Communication:** Listening and communicating are fundamental. According to research, any top sales performers do considerably more listening than they do talking. Sales and marketing are about identifying needs, and to identify needs one has to listen. In addition, the ability to speak more than one language may be helpful for employment in stores in communities where people from various cultures tend to live and shop.

- **Flexibility:** Someone who is able to adjust in an ever-changing global retail marketplace, interact with many people on different levels, perform a wide variety of tasks during the work day, and be resourceful.

- **Decisiveness:** Someone who is self-motivated and self-starting, able to make quick and calculated decisions, follow through with responsibilities, and accept responsibility for the results.

- **Analytical Skills:** Someone who enjoys and excels at solving problems, analyzing data and predicting trends, and establishing priorities, and is familiar with technologically advanced retail management and control tools (including computers).

- **Stamina:** Someone who can perform well under pressure, handle long working hours, often standing, and maintain professional standards under varied work conditions.

If you're interested in a career in retail management, the Federated Department Stores (operates chains including Macy's, Lazarus, and Bloomingdale's, among others) note the following as qualities they look for in executive trainees:

- **Managerial Spirit**—taking ownership and interest in all aspects of running a business

- **Assertiveness**—possessing the energy level necessary for running a profitable business

- **Creativity**—looking at the business and thinking of new and exciting ways to make it better

- **Problem Solving Ability**—analyzing facts and data to manage a multi-million dollar business

- **Confidence**—aggressively pursuing opportunities to maximize their potential

- **Leadership**—motivating and developing others to work together as a team

THE NATIONAL RETAIL FEDERATION'S RETAIL SKILL STANDARDS

The National Retail Federation (NRF), the premier trade organization in retailing in the U.S., has established skills and performance standards for retail sales associates.

Essentially, the NRF-recognized "Professional Sales Associate" is "able to provide product information and services that result in customer purchases, loyalty, and satisfaction." The Professional Sales Associate demonstrates the following characteristics:

1. Has a commitment to retail sales as a career and a profession
2. Takes personal responsibility for achieving workgroup and organizational objectives
3. Focuses on assuring and improving customer satisfaction
4. Takes initiative to build customer base and loyalty
5. Has a thorough knowledge of the company's and competing product lines
6. Understands customer needs and assists with product selection
7. Maintains professional presentation
8. Communicates effectively at all levels, both inside and outside the company

According to the NRF, employees in high performance retail companies:

- take responsibility for the achievement of organizational objectives
- receive high levels of support from the retailer, in terms of training, technology, or organizational arrangement, to achieve these objectives
- clearly see their jobs and those of coworkers as critical to the success of the company as a whole

Professional Sales Associate Key Duties and Tasks

- provide personalized customer service
- initiate customer contact
- build customer relations
- sell and promote products
- determine customer needs
- build the sale
- close the sale

- monitor inventory
- take inventory
- transfer inventory
- maintain appearance of department/store
- maintain stock, selling, and customer service area
- maintain product presentation and displays
- protect company assets
- identify and prevent loss
- follow safety procedures
- work as part of a department/store team
- support coworkers
- create competitive advantage

Personal Qualities Valued By Retailers

The NRF notes the following personal qualities are highly valued by retailers.

- interpersonal skills
- appropriate workplace behavior
- positive demeanor
- ethics
- courtesy
- flexibility
- leadership
- appearance
- decision-making
- stress tolerance
- problem solving
- efficiency
- reliability
- customer service attitude
- judgment
- motivation
- initiative
- confidence
- creativity
- cross-cultural awareness
- responsibility

Professional Sales Associate Knowledge, Skills, and Abilities

The following is a list of knowledge, skills, and abilities identified by sales associates polled by the NRF as critical to their success and ranked according to their importance:

1. problem solving
2. teamwork
3. courtesy
4. people skills
5. listening
6. work habits
7. speaking
8. learning
9. cross-cultural awareness
10. managing resources
11. observing
12. writing
13. locating information
14. applied mathematics
15. applied technology (such as computer skills)
16. reading for information

For more information about the Skills Standards adopted by the National Retail Foundation for the Professional Sales Associate, check out Appendix C.

TECHNOLOGY AND RETAILING

Although retailing professionals are "people persons," technology is a vital part of the day-to-day functions in the retail industry. To succeed in retail, you'll need to become familiar with these tools.

In almost every retail establishment, every sale to every customer requires technology to do tasks that once were handled by hand. State-of-the-art computer information systems and other high-tech processes help retailers cut costs, work more efficiently, and enhance sales. Technology also helps retailers maximize their use of vast information databases that contain customer-specific buying preferences and purchasing information.

Most retail establishments now use scanners and computers instead of old-fashioned manual cash registers. In a store with scanners, a cashier passes a product's Universal Product Code over the scanning device, which transmits the code number to a computer. The computer identifies the item and its price. In other establishments, cashiers manually enter codes into computers, and descriptions of the items and their prices appear on the screen.

By integrating this data with other statistics, retail managers and owners are able to:

- predict more accurately who their customers are
- anticipate what products their customers want to buy
- plan to have products available when customers want to buy them
- know how much customers are willing to pay for the products

Using technology, retailers produce more accurate sales forecasts, and make better decisions about what products to stock on their shelves. In addition, technology has streamlined the ordering, handling, and delivery of products to the store.

Current information technologies in place include scanners/bar coding, computer networks, relational databases, e-mail, and point-of-sale (POS) terminals. From the planning and ordering of merchandise, to receiving inventory, to planning shelf space, to cash and credit processing, new technologies are changing the way retailers do business.

HOW TO BECOME A RETAIL SALES ASSOCIATE

Now that you have some idea what retail sales associates do and what's important in their success, let's explore how you can enter this in-demand field. There is no one standard way to train for a career in retail sales. You can enter and succeed in retail sales by following these steps:

Graduate from high school or earn a GED

A successful career in retail sales requires good English, communication, and math skills. If your school offers a business curriculum or club, take advantage of it. In almost every city, high school students can participate in DECA, a marketing club that guides them in learning about making a successful career in the retail industry. See Appendix A for information on finding, joining, or starting a DECA club in your town. But if you're not in school and haven't earned your high school diploma, get an equivalency degree (GED), which you can do through most adult education centers or community colleges in your area.

Complete a self-evaluation of your interests, skills, and abilities

If you're still in high school, discuss your career goals with your guidance counselor; he or she can help you clarify your goals, evaluate your strengths, choose the training you need, and obtain financial aid. If you are changing careers or just starting a career after being out of school or the work force for a long time, contact your local community college for career counseling; most will help even if you aren't attending classes there. Or, enlist your family and friends to help you identify your talents and abilities and see if you have what it takes to succeed in retail sales.

An experienced counselor can be very helpful; he or she can give you a series of career-related tests and interpret the results. In addition, some local offices of the state employment service offer free counseling. Counselors won't tell you what to do, but they can help guide you in your search for a good career.

However you do your personal inventory, think about your interests and the kinds of things you do well. Divide them by activities you do well that involve people (such as hosting parties, listening, or giving advice), those that involve things (such as planting a garden, repairing a car, or sewing), and those that involve information (such as writing letters, writing computer programs, or paying bills). What skills do you most enjoy using? Write down your skills, gifts and talents, and then prioritize them in order of importance.

List all the jobs you've ever had. Be sure to include summer jobs, volunteer work, and part-time jobs. Include family responsibilities, such as balancing the bank accounts, child or pet care, and home maintenance. Add any freelance or short-term assignments you've ever done, such as selling cookies for a club, or selling tickets to an organization event. Put down anything you've done that shows initiative and interpersonal skills, such as organizing a wedding, traveling, and so forth.

Do the same thing for your education, starting with high school. List the school(s) you've attended, your major course of study (college prep, business education, vocational training, etc.), classes you particularly enjoyed, grades, special awards or honors, and extracurricular activities.

Another area you need to assess in your personal inventory are your work preferences and attitudes. You may want to create a list that answers questions such as:

- Do you prefer working with a team or individually?
- Do you want good benefits and lots of chances for promotion at work?
- Do you want to perform a variety of tasks, or do you prefer doing a few routine tasks?
- Do you have a lot of stamina or strength?
- Do you prefer working indoors or outdoors?

Decide on the kind of product or service you would most enjoy selling

Think about your hobbies and interests. Do you like clothing, electronic equipment, books, gardening supplies? Getting a part-time or summer job doing sales will help you decide what kind of sales environment you like best.

Find a training program that suits your needs

Although entry-level retail sales jobs are available without formal training, employers do value employees who seek out knowledge and complete relevant education and training programs.

The National Retail Federation encourages individuals interested in a retail career to continue their education beyond high school. Whether you pursue an academic or business-related degree, additional education will enhance your value in the job market and the opportunities available to you. Recommended courses include: marketing, communications, finance, management, merchandising, and information systems (computer science). For many of the specialized management positions, a college degree and more specific business administration courses are very useful and may be required. Colleges and universities in every state offer courses in business; many offer degrees in retailing. (Take a look at chapter three to find many of these.)

You'll need to decide how much training you are able and ready to commit to. For example, a certificate program can take up to 18 months; an associate degree requires two years of full-time attendance, and a bachelor's degree takes four years of full-time attendance. It will take longer to earn a degree for part-time students. (See chapter two for detailed information on all these types of programs.)

Every school's admission requirements are unique, but most will have similar guidelines. They all require some kind of formal application or registration process. Each application will have a deadline date and will request information about your educational background. Often they will request scores from standardized college admissions tests, such as the ACT or SAT. Some may require that you submit a written essay explaining your career goals or why you want to be admitted to that school. Whatever the admissions requirements, make sure you follow them exactly. If you have any questions, don't guess, and don't rely on a friend or relative; call the admissions office and get the correct answer.

Obtain financial aid, as needed, if necessary

Once you've decided on the type of training you need, check on the availability of financial aid. Chapter four contains in-depth information on this topic, but here are some tips:

- Don't assume that you won't qualify for some form of financial assistance.
- Make sure you submit your tax forms by April 15.
- Be honest on your application.
- Always turn in your applications during the application period, and before the deadline.
- Start looking for financial aid as soon as possible.

Complete the training program

This takes planning and commitment. If you work part time, or if you are taking care of a family while you're in training, careful time management is important. Employers look down on job applicants who start, but don't finish, something. (See chapter two for help on ways to make sure you succeed during your training program.)

Conduct a job search

As in every industry, retail stores value employees who have experience, but don't be put off if you don't have any. Most employers will consider a motivated and enthusiastic person with good basic skills for an OJT program.

A thorough job search requires preparing and using a resume. Although resumes aren't required for many entry-level retail sales positions, a good resume convinces the reader that you really want the position and that you are worth interviewing. A resume is a marketing brochure. It is a strategy for you to sell yourself to the employer.

Since selling any product or service is all about selling yourself, make sure you see chapter five for advice and examples to help you create your own resume. Remember to keep your resume current, and update your resume whenever you have new information to add. Have an up-to-date resume handy, so that if you find a position you really want, you won't have to dash off a resume in a hurry; rushing can cause embarrassing mistakes.

Succeed in your first job.
See chapter six for helpful tips.

TYPICAL HIRING PROCEDURES

Among most retail stores, the hiring procedures are similar. Applicants typically fill out an application for employment and participate in an interview.

Since it's common to fill out an application at the store where you'll work, remember to dress neatly, as if you are ready and able to go to work immediately. First impressions count! Never dress as if you are just stopping by the store on your way to play tennis, paint the front porch, or go to the beach.

Many employers expect applicants to complete the application form on site, so remember to bring all necessary information with you when you go to apply for a job. Remember to bring a record of your education and work history, including names, addresses, and phone numbers; a photo ID and Social Security card (or other proof that you are eligible to work in the United States); and a list of personal or professional references (including addresses and phone numbers). Try to fill in every blank on the application. Be careful to spell everything correctly, and print all answers as neatly as you can.

Although most employers for entry-level retail sales jobs don't require a resume, if you bring one to attach to the job application, you will make a positive first impression on the employer.

The store manager or human resources representative may speak briefly with you when you turn in your application. Looking sharp and bringing everything with you will impress him or her.

For positions in larger stores, the employer will probably require that you take a drug screening test and a pre-employment physical examination. They will usually conduct a credit history check and complete a criminal background check. Almost all employers, large and small, will screen your references.

At some organizations, you cannot apply for a position unless it has been posted on the job board or if applications have been requested in the want ads or elsewhere. Large companies that hire many sales associates or hire lots of temporary help during busy seasons often use job hotlines so prospective employees can keep up with current openings. Feel free to stop by or call the employer to ask about current or upcoming job openings, and find out what the application procedure requires.

The Application

If you have ever filled out an application for any kind of job, school, or financial aid, the application for an entry-level position in retail sales will be similar. The application will ask for the following information:

* name, address, phone number (work and home/message)
* other name(s), such as a maiden name, you may have used at school or at work
* social security number
* driver's license or other identification number
* information about your present and former work experience, including dates, responsibilities, supervisor's name, and reason for leaving
* skills (such as what office machines you can operate; languages you speak, read, understand fluently; supervisory experience; etc.)
* schedule availability (days, evenings, weekends, part-time or full-time)
* educational background and degrees
* references
* citizenship or work eligibility status
* your need for accommodation to perform the "essential functions" of the job

The application may ask if you have ever been convicted of a criminal offense, or if you have ever received workers' compensation benefits for a job-related industry. If you answer "yes" to either of these questions, you will be asked to provide details.

No question on the application should ask for a prospective employee's race, color, religion, national origin, age, sex, marital status, or disabilities. The application should state that the company is an "Equal Opportunity Employer."

You must sign the application before turning it in. Your signature verifies that all the information is true and correct. The application will state that incorrect information is cause for immediate dismissal. Remember that the employer will verify the information. It's best to be honest. If you don't know how to complete any portion of the application, ask for assistance from the human resource person or store manager.

An employment application will stay in an "active" file in the company human resource or personnel office for up to one year. Small stores operated by the owner may not have a human resources office, and may have a different way of storing applications. It's appropriate for applicants to ask the employer about the application policy. If you really want to work at a particular company, ask to see how often you should check in with them to keep your application on file, how often to update it, and so on.

Employment Agencies

Employment agencies use the same hiring techniques as other companies. You will fill out an application, the agency will check your references, and, depending on the policy of the agency, you may have to take a drug test. The agency may or may not complete a criminal background check or credit check.

Employment agencies make money when they place an employee with a customer's organization. They want to please their customer (the company that needs employees), so they try very hard to find qualified candidates.

For retail sales, most employment agencies hire highly qualified managers and other workers with a particular expertise for advanced positions. You can try temporary help agencies in your area, though, to see if they place workers in entry-level sales positions. Large stores with many workers and a high rate of employee turnover, as well as new stores moving into a new area, sometimes use employment agencies to help them screen applicants, or to hire temporary workers. (Many

Temporary help agencies frequently place workers in non-sales positions, such as stock clerk, custodian, inventory checker, etc., in retail companies. Although these positions don't require customer contact, they can give you a chance to evaluate the company and see if you might like to work there as a sales associate. If you do well, you will impress the employer and improve your chances to be hired into a sales job.

stores use temps for special events or seasonal work, such as during Christmas.) People who can demonstrate they are good temporary workers can often find permanent employment through temporary or seasonal sales jobs.

Co-ops and Internships

Large retail companies often work with high schools and colleges to establish cooperative education ("co-op") and internship programs for promising students. Both are good ways to get valuable experience and training, and are excellent opportunities for any student wanting "real world" experience.

Co-ops

In a co-op experience, students work part time during the school term and take classes on campus part time. Students may or may not earn academic credit for co-op experience. Some co-ops last just a few weeks; others last up to a semester or longer.

In a retail co-op, the store owner, department head, or an experienced employee will teach students how to operate the cash register or make out sales checks. You'll learn about customer service, security, and the store's policies and procedures. Depending on what type of products the store sells, students may receive additional specialized training by manufacturers' representatives.

John Yaegel completed a co-op in retail while in high school. Now a high school counselor in Tenafly, New Jersey, John learned a lot of valuable skills during his co-op experience. "I learned about time management, assuming responsibility, being creative in your work, communicating with others, planning ahead and many others," he said.

Internships

In an internship, a student works in a company for a specified time, such as a few months (the length of a semester) to a year or more. These programs offer students or recent graduates an opportunity to gain valuable work experience and earn academic credit.

Retail organizations prefer to hire student interns during their junior or senior year of college. They don't hire freshman or sophomore students because they invest a great deal of time and money in interns, and companies don't want to invest too much in students they may lose track of before graduation.

Many students who perform well in internships leave with a job offer; these students don't have to worry about job-hunting the last semester of school.

Sample Internship

Here's a sample paid internship experience offered to qualified undergraduate students at the University of Florida.

DESCRIPTION:

Scotty's began in 1924 as a building materials retailer with a single store in Winter Haven, Florida. Today Scotty's has more than 150 locations in Florida, Georgia, and Alabama with over 4,300 associates. Annual sales are $600,000,000 divided into 70% do-it-yourself and 30% professional markets. Corporate headquarters are located on 58 acres in Winter Haven, which includes a million-square-foot automated distribution center. As Scotty's heads into the 21st century, plans call for relocating and remodeling many of our existing stores, as well as opening new stores where there are opportunities.

Retail management interns will be exposed to a broad base of retail experience, including new-hire orientation, store accounting and administrative functions, and sales experience. A program will be provided which combines six store management training modules with actual application of the training materials as outlined below.

Week 1: Attend new-hire orientation class, safety training, and cashier training

Week 2: Complete training module #1—Human Resources 1. (Interviewing skills, drug testing, orientation of new associates, associate training programs)

Week 3: Complete training module #2—Human Resources 2. (Employee appraisals, discipline, benefit programs, and scheduling)

Weeks 4 & 5: Complete training module #3—Front End/Loss Prevention/Audits. (Cash reconciling, refunds, telephone courtesy, loss prevention issues, and audit issues)

Weeks 6 & 7: Complete training module #4—Selling/Product Presentation. (Selling skills, supply ordering, ad preparation, mass displays, plan-o-grams)

Weeks 8 & 9: Complete training module #5—On-Hands Accuracy/Inventory. (Procedures for maintaining and controlling inventory and the taking of physical inventory)

Week 10: Complete training module #6—Contractor Sales/Management Support. (All aspects of quoting, billing, shipping, and servicing contractors)

In addition to money earned in many retail internships, the school awards academic credit for successfully completing the program. This typically requires the student to complete a special project, write a report describing the learning experience, and have the internship supervisor rate the quality of the student's work.

If you decide you want to work for a particular company and would like to learn retail buying, operations, or management, call the human resources department and ask if there is an internship program for students. Even if the answer is "No," you may find out where to send a formal inquiry. Working with an instructor or counselor in your training program, you will be able to propose an intern-

Internships: A "Win-Win" Opportunity to Students and Employers Cecilia Schulz is Associate Director of the Center for Retailing Education and Research at the University of Florida. She places students in retail management internships, some of which pay very well, "up to $10 an hour!" she says.

Schulz points out that internships offer a "win-win" situation to students and employers. Students discover a lot about themselves and about the company, and companies hire competent workers who will become enthusiastic and loyal employees.

According to Schulz, retail interns learn one of four lessons from the internship experience:

♦ I love retailing and love this company

♦ I hate retailing but love this company

♦ I love retailing but hate this company

♦ I hate retailing and I hate this company

ship, explaining how it would benefit the company, the school and yourself, and include a time limit for the internship, such as a summer, a semester, or a year.

Are internships available for high school students? "High school students can and should explore the availability of internships or other experiential learning opportunities," says Larry Sechney, director of Career Services at Kutztown University in Kutztown, Pennsylvania. "The high school student of the next generation would be wise to explore all avenues of opportunity and remember that while knowledge is power, it is the application of that knowledge that makes one powerful."

WHERE RETAIL SALES PROFESSIONALS WORK

Entry-level positions in retail sales are available everywhere, from the smallest town to the largest cities. To find a position you'll be happy with, you need to think about the kind of company where you'll feel most comfortable. To help you, consider these facts:

♦ Retail formats are becoming more and more polarized, with "big box" stores such as Circuit City, Barnes & Noble, WalMart, and others at one end, and "niche retailers" such as FootLocker and Starbucks at the other.

♦ In 1995, according to the National Research Bureau, there were a total of 41,235 shopping centers in the United States. In 1994 there were 294 outlet centers in the U.S., compared to just 183 centers in 1990.

- One-stop shopping is the name of the game. Grocery and department stores are overhauling their businesses to include pharmacies, video rentals, photo processing, and banking, all in one place. As a result, retail stores are now looking for employees who can handle different tasks, and help customers find everything they want.

- Over 92 percent of U.S. retailers own and operate a single store. Yet, single-store retailers account for less than 50 percent of all retail store sales. Just one tenth of one percent of U.S. retailers have more than 100 stores. Fewer than 500 retail chains have over 100 stores, but these chains account for close to one-third of all retail store sales in the United States.

- The majority of retailers are small businesses, with just under 90 percent of all retail companies employing fewer than 20 workers. 98.6 percent of retailers employ fewer than 100 employees and only 1.2 percent of all retailing companies employ between 100 and 499 employees.

CLASSIFYING RETAIL COMPANIES

Many different categories are used to classify retail establishments. One way to look at employers is by size and number of employees.

Large companies

Large companies have more than 500 employees. WalMart, for example, employs more than 500,000 people! Often, sales associates in large department and chain stores develop a specialty, and work in a particular department. These people are expected to become "experts" about a particular type of product, such as women's shoes, men's shoes, or children's shoes, and so on. Or, they become the "expert" in all the products the store sells made by a specific manufacturer or group of manufacturers.

Most large retail employers have formal training programs for management trainees. They usually recruit college graduates for these programs. Because most companies have a "promote from within" policy to retain high-quality workers, exceptional sales associates without a college background may be invited to complete this training as well. Large companies with many retail stores also give employees the chance to work in different cities or states, and even abroad. If you want the opportunity to participate in this type of learning experience and get the chance to learn a wide range of retail skills leading to a career in management, consider looking for a job in a large company.

Medium-size companies

Retail companies with between 100 and 500 employees usually expect their employees to be somewhere between specialists and generalists. They may be expected to work in a specific department and become knowledgeable about a particular product line; at the same time, they should be flexible and able to fill in as needed in other departments in the same store. (Large stores that want to give customers the "feel" of a smaller store often expect their sales associates to be knowledgeable about more than just their own department, as well.)

Medium-size companies may or may not offer formal management training programs to qualified sales associates and college graduates. Usually they have a policy to promote from within. In some companies, learning new skills comes chiefly through on-the-job experience. Consider working in a company like this if this kind of atmosphere appeals to you.

Small companies

Small retail companies with fewer than 100 employees are still the most common kinds of retail sales environments, although bigger stores and chain stores with outlets in many areas are expanding all the time. Small retail stores may have anywhere from one or two employees to nearly a hundred.

In small companies, sales associates usually have to become familiar with every product sold in the store. They typically have to load and unload merchandise from trucks, stock shelves, create and manage store displays, operate the cash register, gift-wrap, and sweep the floor. They may need to deliver merchandise to a customer, make bank deposits, order inventory, or write advertising copy.

Small companies often hire employees without requiring that they have a college education. Training programs in smaller companies are not usually as formal as those in larger companies, but their standards of excellence are often just as high. They recognize excellence and potential in workers early, because the owner or executive works very closely with all employees. In a smaller company, you'll likely learn working at the elbow of a manager or owner. Your employer will give you more responsibilities as he or she sees fit, rather than on a strict timetable.

Working in small companies exposes workers to every aspect of the business quickly, and allows motivated employees to master a wide range of tasks faster than in larger, more departmentalized organizations. If this appeals to you, consider finding a job in a small retail organization.

> Another word about retail stores and training:
>
> Because providing the best service to customers is a high priority for many employ-ers in the highly competitive retail world, employees are often given periodic training to update and refine their skills.

Types of Retail Establishments

In 1994, the U.S. Department of Commerce reported that the two largest segments of retail sales included automobile and food retailers (grocery stores). General merchandise stores, apparel and accessory stores, and discount department stores accounted for about 28% of total 1994 retail sales. Other types of retailing include home furnishings and furniture stores, eating and drinking places, and gasoline service stations. Additional categories include building materials and garden supply stores, household appliance stores, drug stores, liquor stores, book, bicycle, jewelry, and sporting goods stores.

Often described as "small cities," many large chain or department stores offer exciting career paths in almost every aspect of their business. Rather than looking at the size of an employer, it's helpful to look at retailers this way.

- **Department Store:** A store organized into several individual "depart-ments" selling a great variety of merchandise, including men's, women's, and children's apparel, as well as home furnishings and accessories.
- **Discount/Mass Merchandiser:** A self-service store displaying and selling all kinds of merchandise at lower overall profit margins than other retailers.
- **Warehouse Club/Superstore:** A self-service retailer with cash-and-carry check-out operations. These retailers tend to shun advertising, credit purchases, deliveries, and other amenities. The sole draw for consumers is national brands at low prices. Membership may be required.
- **Wholesale Club:** A self-service retailer which offers nationally advertised brand name goods at wholesale prices to businesses and group members only. These stores are warehouse environments, with large open spaces and little, if any, decorations.
- **Factory Outlet:** There are two types of outlet retailers. First, those who use a factory-type location to display and sell clearance merchandise received from other retailers or manufacturers; second, those merchants who use a factory or outlet store location to sell their own goods (excess stock, seconds and returns, etc.) at sharply discounted prices.

- **Specialty Store:** A retail store concentrating on a limited range of merchandise such as jewelry, furniture, books, or men's or women's apparel and accessories.
- **Catalog:** A retailer that displays and sells merchandise that is shown and described in catalogs produced by the retailer's main office. The catalogs are often sent to customers for mail order buying, and used universally in their retail stores.
- **Retailing on the Internet:** The Internet, the world's largest computer network, is quickly becoming retailing's newest marketing medium. Although few actual monetary transactions are taking place on the Net today compared to buying in stores or through catalogs (mostly due to security issues), retailers are taking full advantage of the Internet's vast audience. Several retailers have created World Wide Web sites that let people shop electronically, and provide users with information ranging from store locations and sales promotions to employment opportunities.

A FINAL WORD

"Retailing is a very diverse industry. It's a very 'now,' 'happening' industry that gives you instant and continual feedback on the job that you're doing." So explains Bill Alcorn, Vice President and Controller for JC Penney Co., in Dallas. "Whether you are making decisions on staffing, buying, displaying, etc., you are getting daily feedback on how you're doing.

"Retailing is for people who like to be challenged, for people who want to make decisions right away. It gives you the chance to exercise people skills, as well as decision-making skills. It involves your feel for what's right for your customer; but, it has evolved into a more analytical industry, using systems and technology to forecast, evaluate and sort information to make it meaningful for you. You must be able to handle risk-taking, have self-confidence to talk with, motivate, and work with people. Working for a retailer is for you if you can be flexible, and both proactive and reactive. It's a great choice for those who enjoy change, are a little creative and a bit analytical," Alcorn says.

THE INSIDE TRACK

Who:	Rob Boger
What:	Regional Human Resources Manager, CarMax (a division of Circuit City, Inc.)
Where:	Odenton, Maryland
Education:	Bachelor's degree, business

Insider's Advice

I love retailing with a passion. Sales and retail in general require flexibility. You must be able to find out a way to do business better, and that requires willingness to change. A high energy level and drive are key. Communicating with other people is crucial in retail. You must enjoy people and interacting with them. If you're not committed to retail you won't be a success. You have to have a customer-service orientation.

In my job I do mostly associate relations: I help develop associates' careers, discipline associates, and help stores with serious personnel problems. My retailing experience helps me listen to associates and know what the problems are. I help managers and associates see both sides. My listening skills as an HR manager are the same as from doing retail sales. When you're a salesperson, you listen when a customer tells you they have a family of four; and you know a little car isn't what they need. I love seeing associates develop, and helping the manager perform better. I help people understand what it takes to perform better, and then watch the light bulb click on. I worked with one manager who was concerned about a sales associate who was underselling. We discussed ways to help motivate the associate, and she learned ways to help the associate be successful. As a result, she's had the best sales team for three months in a row.

Insider's Take on the Future

Although I predict we'll see more use of technology in retail, customers still want someone to help them, to ring up the sale. People still want to go in and touch merchandise, kick the tires, test-drive it. You can't do that on the Internet.

I enjoy field operations; eventually I may want a corporate environment. I would like to get my masters degree, but I don't have time right now.

In retail, hard work, dedication and general intelligence will get you anywhere. Planning and organizing will help you juggle the work environment. Jobs require multi-tasking; if you enjoy that, you'll be very successful. Every job in retail is juggling.

CHAPTER | 2

This chapter describes the training that will help you launch a successful retail sales career. You'll find tips on how to evaluate retail training programs and several sample course descriptions from training programs across the country. Then you'll get advice on studying for exams, taking notes, networking with classmates, getting to know your instructors, and using the career counseling or job placement office.

ALL ABOUT TRAINING PROGRAMS

Although you may be able to get a job as a retail sales associate without formal training, training and education will give you a competitive advantage in getting a position that will lead to raises in salary, promotions, and more challenging assignments.

Stanley Guss has over 30 years of experience as a retail manager, human resources executive, and executive recruiter. He is president of Bentley Associates in Scarborough, New York, and operates the Retail Job Mart on the Internet at http://www.retailjobmart.com. He notes that many careers in retail start during school years. "You can start out as floor sales while you're in school," he says. "When you graduate, if you have been a good performer, the company may move you into an executive training program. You become a lead person, then an associate manager, and go on from there."

Regardless of the level of education they pursue, people who want to advance in retail complete business courses, including accounting, administration, marketing, management, and sales. Courses in psychology, sociology, and communications are helpful.

MAKING DECISIONS ABOUT TRAINING

Deciding on a training program is challenging. If you didn't complete the personal assessment described in chapter one, now is a good opportunity to review it and finish any parts you need to. When you've completed it, use your answers to consider the following questions. Even though you may not know the answers yet, these questions can help you decide which training program is best for you, and can help you clarify your career goals.

- Do I need a job right away, or can I wait and get the experience or knowledge I need through more education first?
- What kind of training or degree do I want to complete?
- How long am I willing to spend in school before getting a job?
- Would an internship or work-study program benefit me?
- What kind of financial aid can I receive from the school? Can I get enough to attend an expensive four-year university program?
- How much will tuition, books, tools, housing, and other expenses cost?
- What kind of lifestyle do I want while I'm going to school?
- Will my family and friends support my decision about training and education?

Your budget and the cost of the training program will influence your decision to go to school part time and work part time, apply for financial aid, or participate in work-study programs. It will also determine what kind of college or training institution you attend.

You also need to ask yourself these questions:

- What schools are in my area? Do they have training programs that help me meet my goal?
- Are there programs in schools where I hope to live and work after I complete my training?
- To get the education or training I want, will I need to relocate?

Can you afford to relocate to complete training? An appropriate program may be in your state but not in your community. If you move to a different state to attend school, expect the tuition to be much more than tuition for a state resident. If you move, you'll need to find housing; can you afford a place of your own, or live with roommates? Can you live on campus? Many smaller colleges and most community colleges don't have dormitories for students.

HOW TO EVALUATE TRAINING PROGRAMS

Vocational schools, as well as colleges and universities, are businesses. In order to make money, they need to sell their services to students. As someone considering a career in retail sales, think of a school as an "education store": can you get what you want or need by "shopping" there and buying what they are selling?

Before applying to or enrolling in any school or college, remember that its brochures, Web site, catalog, and admissions personnel are there to advertise what's good about it, and to persuade you to spend money to go there. As a consumer, you should carefully study, evaluate, and compare schools, just as if you were buying a new car.

One of the characteristics you should look for in any school or program you are considering is whether it is *accredited*. Accreditation recognizes schools and academic programs that provide a high level of performance, integrity, and quality. Schools and colleges undergo the accreditation process voluntarily. Three national and six regional accrediting agencies grant accreditation in their jurisdictions throughout the United States. In addition, some professional associations accredit specialized programs. These organizations accredit an institution based on the school's curriculum, student and staff ratios, and other criteria established by the agency. Accreditation assures students and employers that the school and its programs offer current, high-quality courses taught by qualified instructors. Appendix B provides information about contacting accrediting organizations.

Here's a list of criteria you can use to evaluate each school you are considering. Use these items, or make a list of your own, and rate each program according to your priorities and needs.

- setting (urban, suburban, rural)
- centralized campus or large campus across large area
- size of student body
- teacher-student ratio (large classes or small)

- coed or same-sex campus
- work-study on campus available, or part-time jobs off campus
- access to cultural, religious, or athletic activities
- child care available
- public transportation available
- services for students with disabilities
- services for older or nontraditional students
- tutoring available
- state-of-the-art technology (laboratory equipment, internet access, on-campus e-mail, etc.)
- affordable housing available
- scholarships and other financial aid available
- public or private school
- types of certificates or degrees offered
- accreditation
- specialized retail program or general business/marketing program
- length of training programs
- job placement program for graduates
- retail and management links with private industry and business that help keep program current, offer internships, place graduates, etc.
- percentage of graduating students placed in retail positions

Try to visit the school before applying. Talk to the school's guidance counselors, faculty, and students and try to get a feel for the atmosphere. Try to get names and phone numbers of people who have graduated from the school and the retail program, if available. These alumni are usually very valuable and honest about their experience, and can tell you how much attending the school helped them in their career.

Be ready to ask questions about the school and surrounding community, especially about work opportunities and other details you may not find in the promotional materials. See if the school seems like a good fit for your criteria.

Depending on the school and its admissions requirements, you may need to answer questions during this evaluation process. When you prepare for an on-campus visit, make sure that you do the following:

- Make an appointment to visit the admissions office, the guidance office, and the office of the director of the program you're interested in (such as the retail careers program).

- Try to make your appointments far enough apart (at least 15 minutes between the end of one appointment and the beginning of the next) so you have time to find the next office (if you don't have someone escorting you from place to place) and to think about what you have learned.

- Record the names of the persons who scheduled each appointment for you, as well as the names of the persons you will meet with. Get directions to each office you'll visit. Ask the office to send you a map and parking instructions, as needed.

- Bring a copy of your high school transcript or permanent record card to take with you.

- Include a list of honors or awards you earned in school, at work, or in the community.

- Know your college entrance exam (ACT, SAT, PSAT) scores in case you are asked about them.

- Bring a notepad and pen or pencil to write notes about questions you ask, questions you answered, and other things you'll want to think about later.

- Arrive early for your appointments so you can spend some time people-watching and getting a sense of the school and its environment.

Entrance Requirements

Depending on which program and school you want to attend, you may have to complete entrance and placement exams. These tests evaluate your reading, writing, and math skills. Keep in mind that even if you score low in one area or another, it may not disqualify you from attending the school; instead, it may mean that you will be required to complete a remedial class to beef up your skills before you are ready to succeed in higher-level coursework.

Length of Retail Training Programs

Training programs for retail sales associates range from in-house courses offered to staff by employers to advanced degrees completed at four-year colleges and graduate schools. In addition, training for many skills needed in retail sales positions is offered in high schools, public vocational-technical centers, and community colleges.

> ### Management Training Programs
>
> Many national retail chains have formal training programs for management trainees that include both classroom and in-store training. Training may last from one week to a year or more, as many retail organizations require their trainees to gain experience during all shopping seasons. Ordinarily, classroom training includes such topics as interviewing and customer service skills, employee and inventory management, and scheduling. Management trainees may be placed in one specific department while training on the job, or they may be rotated through several departments to gain a well-rounded knowledge of the store's operation. Training programs for franchises are generally extensive, covering all functions of the company's operation, including promotion, marketing, management, finance, purchasing, product preparation, human resource management, and compensation. College graduates can usually enter management training programs directly. For non-graduates, people with work experience in the organization have the best chance of getting accepted.

How do you determine which training path to pursue? Keep these facts in mind:

- The more formal education you have, the higher level of entry jobs you're likely to qualify for.
- The more education you have, the better your opportunities for advancing into supervisory or management positions.
- Unless you want to be a "professional student" and can afford to be one, you want to aim toward accomplishing your educational goals as quickly as possible, without sacrificing the quality of the education.

WHAT KIND OF TRAINING SHOULD I AIM FOR?

Depending on the amount of schooling you've already completed and your long-term career goals, there are different types of training programs that can prepare you to be a competitive player in retailing.

High School Programs for Nongraduated Students

If you are still in high school or have left school and haven't earned a GED yet, and you are still under 20 years old, your local school district may have a marketing or business education program that you should check out. Or, you may be eligible to participate in a cooperative education ("co-op") program. Chapter one describes co-op programs.

Certificate Programs

Certificate programs usually take less than one year to complete, but some may take one year, or even two. Graduates receive a certificate of completion. In certificate programs, any general education requirements are meant to directly support the occupational study. In retailing, some certificate programs are self-paced; they offer a combination of classroom and computer or video-based classes designed for people who want to progress at their own speed.

Sample Certificate Program: Fashion Merchandising

Course Requirements		Quarter Credit Hours
Major Courses:		
F101	Introduction to the Fashion Business	4
F106	Textiles Analysis	3
F108	Visual Merchandising	2
F205	Buying Procedures	3
F208	Merchandise Planning and Control	3
F223	Product Knowledge	3
F270	Fashion Field Study	2
V103	Color and Design	3
Business Courses		
B100	Business Organization and Management	4
B136	Professional Selling	3
B212	Advertising and Promotion	4
B220	Placement Seminar	1
CA101	Computer Essentials	2
CA110	Computer Applications	3
OA101	Keyboarding	2
OA201	Keyboarding Skills Laboratory*	1
General Education Courses		
E101	English Composition I	3
E102	English Composition II	3
E111	Oral Communication	3
G100	Freshman Seminar	1
GS110	Group Dynamics	3
GS141	Psychology	4
Free Elective		

Electives

B115	Principles of Accounting	4
B210	Internship	3
B231	Business Law	4
B242	Principles of Management	4
F102	Fashion Show Coordination	2
F104	Retail Management	3
F233	Apparel Design and Illustration	2

Others as posted

62 credit hours required for graduation

* Students who demonstrate the ability to type 40 WPM can test out of Keyboarding Skills Laboratory.

Associate Programs

An associate degree program requires attending classes for at least two academic years (four semesters), and completing at least 60 semester credits, or 90 quarter credits. Associate degree programs are available in community and junior colleges, some four-year colleges, and some technical or trade schools. Entrance requirements usually include a high school diploma or GED, and often entrance and placement exams. In some cases, qualified high school students can take college-level courses leading to an associate degree. In an associate degree program, about half the required courses are in general education or liberal arts (math, English, science, history, etc.), and half are in your selected major, such as business, retail management, or fashion merchandising.

Sample Associate Degree Program in Retail Management

Description: The Retail Management major combines theory with practical experience in such techniques as sales forecasting, buying, merchandising, point-of-sale advertising, sales promotion, inventory control, and achievement of profit as well as various management functions and positions. Students may also use these skills in some entrepreneurial endeavor.

Course Requirements	Quarter Credit Hours

Major Courses

F104	Retail Management	3
F205	Buying Procedures	3
F208	Merchandise Planning and Control	3
B130	Principles of Marketing	4
B136	Professional Selling	3
B212	Advertising and Promotion	4
B242	Principles of Management	4
B290	Retail Management Internship	5

Business Courses

B100	Business Organization and Management	4
B110	Mathematics for Business	4
B121	Financial Accounting I	4
B220	Placement Seminar	1
B231	Business Law	4
CA101	Computer Essentials	2
CA110	Computer Applications	3
CA202	Integrated Software Skills	1
OA101	Keyboarding	2

General Education Courses

E101	English Composition I	3
E102	English Composition II	3
E103	English Composition III	3
E111	Oral Communication	3
G100	Freshman Seminar	1
GS110	Group Dynamics	3
GS134	Macroeconomics	4
GS141	Psychology	4
Humanities Elective		3
Mathematics/Science Elective		4
Free Electives		5

Business Electives

F106	Textiles Analysis	3
F108	Visual Merchandising	2
F223	Product Knowledge	3

F225	Product Development	3
V103	Color and Design	3
B122	Financial Accounting II	4
B125	Managerial Accounting	4
B131	Consumer Behavior	3
B246	Management Seminar	2
B249	Human Resources Management	4
B255	Entrepreneurship	4
IB101	International Business	4
IB220	International Trade	4
IB230	International Marketing	4
IB250	International Sourcing	3
IB260	International Business Seminar	2
TT101	Travel and Tourism	3
CA222	Advanced Spreadsheets	2
CA224	Advanced Database Management Systems	2
CA290	Multimedia and the World Wide Web	2

Others as posted

90 quarter credit hours are required for graduation

In the sixth quarter most courses are offered only during the late afternoon and early evening so as to not interfere with internships.

Bachelor's Degree Programs

The baccalaureate, or bachelor's degree, program combines courses in your major field (such as marketing, finance, management, etc.) with general education in a four-year curriculum at a college or university. A high school diploma or GED is usually required for admission into a bachelor's degree program; in some cases, qualified high school students can take college-level courses leading to a bachelor's degree before receiving their high school diploma.

Many colleges and universities have selective admissions criteria, which means they tend to be more competitive than shorter education and training programs. Generally, applicants must have acceptable scores on college admission and placement tests such as the SAT or ACT, and an acceptable high school grade point average (GPA).

Sample Bachelor's degree Program in Retail Management

Required Courses—18 hours

Title		Semester Credit Hours
MRKTG 3153	Principles of Retailing	3
MRKTG 3413	Principles of Advertising	3
MRKTG 3163	Retail Merchandising	3
MRKTG 3213	Retail Buying	3
MRKTG 4423	Consumer and Market Behavior	3
MRKTG 4453	Retail Management	3

Select 6 hours from the following:

DESCI 3113	Business Statistics II	3
MRKTG 4113	Marketing Research	3
MNGMT 3313	Personnel Management	3
MNGMT 4263	Small Business Management	3
MRKTG 2313	Salesmanship	3
MRKTG 3113	Credit and Collections	3
MRKTG 4433	Purchasing and Materials Management	3

Approved workshops, seminars, institutes

*Include electives and required general education courses to bring total number of hours to equal 124 semester hours

Sample Course Outline

Here is a sample course syllabus, or outline, from the University of Florida College of Business. Wherever you decide to get your training and education, course outlines such as this provide valuable information concerning what's covered during the class, reading or other class assignments, guest speakers, and so on.

MAR 4905: Business Career Planning Spring 1998

The goal for this course is to help guide students with a business degree in deciding upon a career. Guest speakers will discuss topics that the student will encounter at some point early in a career. The course should be used to gain valuable information about careers in business. The presentations will instigate discussion about goals within business careers and ways to achieve those goals.

Date	Topic	Assignment
JAN 9	ORIENTATION	Read the syllabus!
JAN 16	CAREER PATHS FINANCE Joel Houston, Professor of Finance	Appendix A; pg 373–374
JAN 23	DYNAMICS OF SUCCESSFUL LEADERSHIP Betsy Crockett, Area Manager, Gulf Coast Stores, Gayfers	Ch 26, pg 266–274
JAN 30	INTERVIEWS/WHAT YOU AND THEY SHOULD EXPECT Sears Resume due! Bob Wery, Director of College Relations	Ch 14, pg 122–140
FEB 6	MAKING PRESENTATIONS THAT ARE HEARD Selman Hershfield, Toastmasters International	no reading
FEB 13	ENTREPRENEURSHIP–The Benefits, The Drawbacks Juan Gramage, Owner of Do Art and Interetail	no reading
FEB 20	CAREER PATHS IN MANAGEMENT Heather Elms, Department of Management	Ch 24, pg 230–234
FEB 27	HOW TO MOTIVATE PEOPLE Mark O'Neil, Vice President and General Manager, CarMax	pg 302–305
MAR 6	CAREER PATHS Mary Beth Fritz, Department of DIS	no reading
MAR 20	COMMUNICATION SKILLS IN BUSINESS Bob Cramer, Associate Director for Program Development, Career Resource Center	Ch 25, pg 244–265
MAR 27	CONFLICT MANAGEMENT Mason Allen, Sr. VP Merchandising (retired), Stein Mart, Awareness Marketing Group (consultant)	Ch 23, pg 205–230
APR 3	SURFING THE NET FOR CAREERS IN BUSINESS Dick Hughes, Director of Instructional Services	Ch 9 & 10 pg 62–86
APR 10	CAREER PATHS IN MARKETING Bart Weitz, Chairperson, Department of Marketing	Appendix A pg 374, 380 & 389
APR 17	MANAGING LIFE, FINDING BALANCE, AND SUCCEEDING IN BUSINESS Bob White, Director of Training and Development, Mitchells Formal Wear	Ch 34 & 35

Internal Training Programs

In addition to academic and vocational programs, many large retail organizations provide new and experienced employees with structured training classes. These courses address topics such as the company's history and philosophy, product and service information, loss prevention strategies, sales and marketing techniques, and more.

Tips on Applying to Programs

♦ Apply as early as you can. Complete the application, submit transcripts as instructed, and make sure the school receives official copies of any college entrance or placement exams required for admission. Check with an admissions counselor or your high school guidance counselor for more information about admission requirements, schedules, fees, and so on.

♦ Make sure you arrange to apply for financial aid or to take placement exams as soon as you can. If you get behind on these important steps, it may delay or prevent you from being admitted to the program of your choice, or from the courses you need.

♦ Pay tuition and fees before the deadline. You may not be able to enroll in your desired courses until your financial obligations are met on or before the date specified on the registration form.

MAKING THE MOST OF THE TRAINING PROGRAM

After you commit yourself to a training program, it's in your best interest to excel. Use the tips below to get the most out of your training program.

How to Study for Exams

Studying is crucial if you want to succeed in your training. And in retailing, you'll need good study skills and habits to stay on top of product knowledge, company policies and procedures, and all the other information you need to stay ahead of the competition.

Erik Gordon directs the Center for Retailing Education and Research at the University of Florida (Gainesville). He notes that good grades show potential employers that you have discipline and a commitment to doing well. "The excuse that classes don't matter because they're not 'real world' doesn't work; employers want people who will do well with every task that is assigned to them, not just with tasks they find interesting."

Exams are your instructor's way of measuring how much of the information presented in class or gathered by completing course assignments you have learned. Instructors use a variety of exam styles to assess their students' learning. Some tests use multiple choice or true and false items, in which the correct answer is usually pretty easy to identify for students who have studied the material and thought about the content. Short-answer and essay questions require students to write the answer to questions; you really need to be familiar with the course material to do well on these types of items. Usually, your instructor will tell you what kind of questions to expect, so you can study appropriately.

Some experts suggest that students should study one hour each week for every hour spent in class. For example, if you take a class for one hour on Monday, Wednesday and Friday, for a total of three hours each week, you should expect to study at least three hours a week for that class. Others recommend that you study two hours a week for each hour spent in class. What's right for you will depend on how easily the content comes to you; plan on spending more time on the more challenging courses.

Regardless of how much time you spend studying, budget your time so you don't need to cram the night before the test. Studies show students study less effectively, retain less information, and perform worse on exams when they are tired than when they are rested and alert.

Concentration is vital for effective studying. To make studying easier, apply these tips:

- Set up an area with your course materials, paper, writing implements (including pens or pencils, as well as highlighter pens for marking written materials), and sticky notes.
- Always use adequate lighting to see what you're doing and avoid eye strain.
- Prevent (or tune out) distractions from anyone in your study area. Ask your roommate, family, or friends to respect your study time by staying away (or at least by keeping quiet). Unplug the phone or use the answering machine to avoid chatting during study time.
- Take breaks of about five minutes for every hour of study. Stand, stretch your legs and fingers, take your eyes off the computer monitor. Taking regular breaks will help keep you fresh.

If you review your notes, keep up on reading assignments, study with others as needed, and get tutoring or extra help when needed, you should be prepared for exams. Remember always to read test instructions carefully and listen to your instructor's directions.

How to Take Notes in Class

Taking regular, clear, and concise notes in class helps many people concentrate on the instructor and remember what happened during class later. Even if you use a tape recorder in class (a very good approach if you remember best by listening, if you aren't a very fast writer, or can never read your handwriting!), taking notes will help you be a better student.

Reviewing notes regularly is an excellent habit to develop. By checking your notes the same day that you took them lets you add or correct any information that you didn't have time to write down before, organize your pages, and highlight key points. It's also a great way to help the material sink in, which will make studying for exams easier.

There are a number of note-taking methods available. Find an approach that works for you, using some of the following tips, or create your own method.

In the **outline method**, classify information as a major idea, subset of the major idea, or a detail. Traditionally, broad concepts are noted on the left margin of the page, marked with a Roman numeral (I, II, II, etc.). Subheadings are marked beneath the major heading with letters (A,B,C, etc.) and details are marked beneath the subheading using Arabic numerals (1, 2, 3, etc.); even finer points are shown using lowercase letters (a, b, c, etc.).

Here's a sample:

I. Taking Notes
    A. Types of note-taking methods
        1. Outline
           a) use hierarchy of numerals and letters (Roman, capitals, Arabic) to write notes from the broad to the narrow

In the **columnar method**, students use two or three columns to separate the major concepts and the related subheadings and details. To use this approach, use lined notebook paper. Enter major ideas to the left of the vertical line, more detailed information to the right of the line. Or, turn your paper sideways and make vertical lines to mark your columns.

Here's a sample, using three columns:

Taking Notes	Methods	Outline: use hierarchy of numerals and letters (Roman, capitals, Arabic) to write notes from the broad to the narrow. Columnar: use two or three columns . . .

Some people use the informal diagramming method of note-taking. This approach lets you place information inside boxes or circles where you determine they'll mean the most to you, and link main ideas to subheadings and details using arrows, dotted lines, or other symbols to mark relationships between them. Here's a sample, where the main concept is enclosed in a circle, and the subheadings and details are bound in boxes:

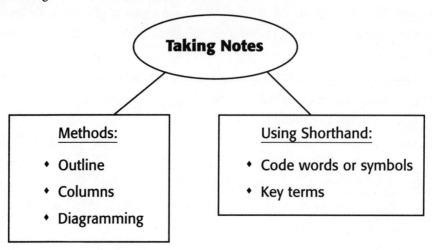

A Word about Shorthand

Unless you have amazingly fast (and clear) handwriting, you're bound to miss some of what you hear in your classes. Instructors sometimes speak very fast, or use terms and jargon that are unfamiliar to you (not to mention difficult to spell!). Also, constantly writing out long words that you may hear frequently in class, such as *merchandising*, or common words such as *with* will wear you out. Some people drop vowels in common words, so *retail* becomes *rtl*, or use abbreviations, so *assistant buyer* becomes *A.B.* Others use traditional shorthand, such as the @ sign to mean *about, concerning*, or a quantity (such as *@500*), or *w/* for *with*, and so on.

Don't bother writing complete sentences in taking notes. Drop articles, such as "the," "a," or "it." What's important is that you understand the concept and significance of what you write down, not that others can.

Studying with Other Students

Make friends and study with people in your classes. They may have heard something important that you may have missed. They may have a better understanding about a particular subject than you have. Or, you may be able to share your knowledge or comfort with a subject with someone who can use your help. Either way, it's a great way to learn and establish worthwhile networking relationships with people who are in the same boat as you.

Getting to Know the Instructor

Peers can give you moral support and can become valuable friends. But never underestimate the value of getting to know, and getting known by, your instructors. Take advantage of your instructors' office hours or free periods, and let them see you as a person with goals and ambitions, not as just a body taking up space in class. Approach teachers with questions that weren't asked in class. Seek their advice on academic or career planning, industry trends, job hunting, and so on.

Using the Career Planning and Placement Office

The career planning and placement office of your school is a treasure trove of information, advice, and support for students. Career counselors help students clarify their goals, assist in developing or critiquing resumes and cover letters, refer students to area employers seeking competent employees, and more. Many schools coordinate job and career fairs through the career center office. Many centers have a career information library, offer workshops and seminars on career planning topics, coordinate student internships, and more.

A FINAL WORD

If you are planning to attend college to give yourself an edge over the competition to launch your retail career, you will need to organize yourself for applying for college and financial aid. (For some helpful tips, check out the "College Admission Calendar" at Peterson's Web site, located at www.petersons.com/resources/calendar.html.) By setting goals and gathering information early in the training and education game, you will learn valuable skills in prioritizing and carrying out key tasks that will help you succeed in whatever training your pursue.

THE INSIDE TRACK

Who:	Mike Wright
What:	Operations Manager for American Stores, Osco Drug Division
Where:	Champaign, Illinois
Education:	Bachelor's degree

Insider's Advice

I have been in retail management for eight years. The retail workplace is a very people-oriented work area. One must be able to communicate with customers and employees on a daily basis. Also, retail stores reflect their community. A store in the suburbs will be totally different than a store in the city, even if the same company runs them. A manager needs to be able to relate to the people in the neighborhood since these people will be their customers and employees.

When you look for a position, look for a company that cares about its workers and treats them with respect and equality. Also, look for a company that has high standards. It's hard to work in a store that is cluttered, messy, and dark. Basically, if you wouldn't shop there, then you probably wouldn't want to work there. Also, watch the employees. If they are happy and being productive then the company probably trained them well and has good benefits. A nice clean store, with good lighting, employees that don't resent being there, and customers who are having a pleasant shopping experience are good signs of a pleasant work environment.

Insider's Take on the Future

The one thing that remains constant in the retail industry is "change." Companies are always introducing new technologies designed to help the employee work better and help the customer have a pleasant shopping experience. Many things are becoming automated. Products are scanned at the register, orders are transmitted via modem over the phone lines, training courses are being given via two-way teleconferencing.

All this new technology allows the job to get done using fewer employees. Payroll is the biggest and most controllable expense at the store level. Lower payroll expenses allow the store to keep prices down and stay competitive. Unfortunately, this is the cause of a lot of stress for the worker, who now has more responsibilities and workload.

CHAPTER | 3

This chapter describes the different types of retailing-related training programs that are available. You'll learn about appropriate majors for retailing careers, and you'll see several sample course descriptions. Then you'll find a state-by-state directory of schools that offer programs in a retailing-related field. You can contact each school directly to get more information and request applications for the programs that interest you.

DIRECTORY OF RETAIL TRAINING PROGRAMS

Once you've decided that you want to get a retailing education to get a winning edge on the competition, you need to find a program that meets your standards and expectations. This chapter will show you how to do just that. Let's begin by reviewing the variety of kinds of programs that are available; these will give you a jump on the competition for good jobs in the retail industry.

MAJORS APPROPRIATE FOR CAREERS IN RETAIL

Retailers will tell you that the qualities or knowledge that make someone successful in retailing aren't limited to a few college majors. In fact, many retail executives will tell you that colleges aren't especially good at training people in retail sales techniques, and they welcome people from varied educational backgrounds as long as they have other important qualities.

TYPES OF PROGRAMS

Program or Degree	Content
High School Programs for Non-Graduated Students	Marketing education or general business training; "co-op" education/work experience
Certificate Program	One year or less
Associate Degree Program	Two years; majors in areas such as retail management, fashion merchandising, marketing, business
Bachelor's Degree	Four years; majors in areas such as marketing, management, finance, etc.

Retailers look for people with creativity, analytical skills, flexibility, good interpersonal skills, and the ability to take risks and make decisions. They also appreciate individuals who have demonstrated the ability to study, learn and absorb a broad body of knowledge. That's why they value people with training, particularly people with a college degree.

Does this mean that it makes no difference what you major in? No, not really. If you know that you want to apply your talents in a retail environment, having a good grounding in business theory and practice is very helpful. Let's review some of the more common majors available in technical schools, colleges and universities that will provide a good foundation for a successful retail career.

Management

Students who major in management, especially taking courses emphasizing retail management, develop their skills and knowledge in the management functions of planning, organizing, leading, and controlling. These tools help graduates know how to acquire, distribute, use and maintain the organization's resources. Course work exposes students to actual problem situations that may be encountered by managers.

Students may also opt to emphasize courses in human resource management, organization management, or production/operations management. When combined with appropriate courses, students create an educational program that will enable them to perform effectively in any work environment.

Retail Merchandising

This major equips students with the underlying fundamentals of merchandising theory, and the ability to mathematically translate that theory into the planning factors that govern the day-to-day operations of a profitable retail enterprise. Students learn theoretical concepts, such as the cost method of inventory, and solve realistic problems that expose the theory's benefits and weaknesses. They acquire the mathematical knowledge necessary to understand and use merchandising theories in real-life instances.

Marketing

Marketing is the process that delivers want-satisfying products and services in both domestic and international markets. Marketing includes activities such as planning and development, pricing, advertising, selling, promotion, research, and distribution. The curriculum examines marketing management problems, policies, and practices as well as economic, cultural, environmental, and political forces affecting marketing performance.

Fashion Merchandising

Fashion merchandising students learn about fabrics, apparel design and construction, fashion trends, and retail business. This degree prepares students for employment in areas such as fashion sales, specialty shop management, accessory coordination and fashion buying.

Finance

The finance and accounting curriculum in colleges is designed to prepare students for careers managing the financial assets of the employer. Students learn how to organize and analyze financial data, make investment decisions and recommendations, and more.

Bill Alcorn is vice president and Controller at JC Penney Co., in Dallas, Texas. He earned a bachelor's degree in Finance. "I've been with Penney 26 years, starting part-time in college," he recalls. "I interviewed with many organizations for positions in accounting. I decided I didn't want to sit in an office and churn out numbers. I wanted to work with people, face different challenges, travel, have contact with all kinds of people. I found what I was looking for in Penney's auditing department. Retailing is a people business regardless of what part you are in. A huge part of what I do is to be responsive to people."

WHAT IF I DON'T WANT TO MAJOR IN A BUSINESS DISCIPLINE?

Many successful retailers majored in non-business areas. If there's a subject—from anthropology to zoology—that fascinates you, but you're still aiming for a career in retailing you should take courses that give you a background in the general principles of business, as well as its specialized vocabulary.

According to Erik Gordon, Director of the Center for Retailing Education and Research at the University of Florida, "Even retailers with comprehensive in-house training programs find it easier to train students who understand how business works. Retailers without extensive training programs also look for people who have completed coursework in retailing."

SAMPLE COURSE DESCRIPTIONS

Here are several sample course descriptions, taken from the catalogue of Rochester (Minnesota) Community College. These courses are part of the school's associate degree programs in retail merchandising. The descriptions include the course title, a synopsis of material covered, the number of hours spent in class each week, the number of credits earned, prerequisites, and the quarters when the course is offered (as available). These descriptions provide an idea of the kinds of courses you should look for in your retailing education.

Course Descriptions
Principles of Marketing

Provides the student with a general introduction to marketing analysis, planning, decision making and program implementation. Students gain an understanding of the principles of marketing and their interrelationship through a computerized business marketing simulation and development of a formal market plan.

> 4 hours per week
>
> 4 credits
>
> Prerequisite: None
>
> Quarters offered: Winter, Spring

Human Relations

Problems and situations employees at all levels of an organization will encounter, as they interact with co-workers, quality of work life, group cooperation, leadership, change, and current organization issues are main topics of study and discussion.

> 3 hours per week
>
> 3 credits
>
> Prerequisite: None

Supervision

Principles and techniques of supervision which may be applied in planning, directing and evaluating the work of others.

3 hours per week

3 credits

Prerequisite: None

Retailing

A fundamental view of the retail industry including site selection, store organization, layout and design, consumer behavior, buying, selling, promotional activity, store services and personnel management.

3 hours per week

3 credits

Prerequisite: None

Salesmanship

Retail store salesmanship including sales personality, why people buy, approaching the customer, determining the customer's wants and needs, presenting the merchandise, sales, demonstrations, merchandise information, overcoming objections, closing the sale and suggestion selling.

3 hours per week

3 credits

Prerequisite: None

Principles of Management

Students will gain an understanding of the basic functions managers perform. They will assess the challenges faced by managers in today's business environment and learn how the concepts and applications of management relate to the group and individual behavior within the organization.

4 hours per week

4 credits

Prerequisite: None

Quarters offered: Winter, Spring

Introduction to Retail Merchandising

An introduction to the field of retail merchandising with an emphasis on men's, women's, and children's apparel and accessories, including the economic, sociological, and psychological factors that influence buying patterns of consumers.

4 hours per week

4 credits

Prerequisite: None

Quarters offered: Fall

(continued)

Course Descriptions, *Continued*
Visual Merchandising

A study of total visual presentation of merchandise to the consumer. Elements, principles and philosophies of display are examined with the goals of achieving a desired image or impact.

> 4 hours per week plus scheduled lab work required
>
> 4 credits
>
> Prerequisite: None
>
> Quarters offered: Fall, Spring

Store Management

Development of management skills for retail stores of varying sizes.

> 4 hours per week
>
> 4 credits
>
> Prerequisite: None

Retail Buying

Merchandising selection and control in department and specialty stores, especially soft goods and other fashion related items. Areas included will be budgeting, assortment planning, managing inventory, and buying for resale.

> 4 hours per week
>
> 4 credits
>
> Prerequisite: None

Merchandise Planning and Control

Merchandising selection and control of a retail department to include budgeting, assortment planning, inventory and buying plans.

> 4 hours per week
>
> 4 credits
>
> Prerequisite: None

Retail Merchandising Seminar

An examination of topics of current interest to merchandising students. Speakers are brought in from the field to share their background and knowledge.

> 1-3 credits
>
> Prerequisite: None

Internship

Work experience program designed to help merchandising students apply classroom information on the job. Designed to make the work experience a learning experience so the student will be able to advance into a management position.

> 50 hours per credit
>
> 3-5 credits
>
> Prerequisite: Sophomore standing in the Retail Merchandising Program

DIRECTORY OF RETAILING-RELATED TRAINING PROGRAMS

As you've seen so far in this chapter, there is a wide variety of training programs available to help you prepare for your career in retailing. This section provides a representative listing of schools in each state that offer retailing-related training programs. Not every institution that offers a program could be listed here due to space limitations. However, this listing should get you started.

The colleges and universities in this directory have been culled from several sources, including the National Retail Federation and the American Collegiate Retailing Association. These schools offer degrees in retailing, merchandising, retail management, retail marketing, retail sales, and/or fashion apparel merchandising. The schools are listed in alphabetical order within each state. Although the institutions included in this directory are not endorsed or recommended by the author or by LearningExpress, this listing should help you begin your search for an appropriate program. Always contact the schools you are considering for current information on program requirements and areas of specialization before you apply.

ALABAMA

Auburn University at Auburn
Room 202 Mary Martin Hall
Auburn 36849
334-844-4000; Fax: 334-844-6436

Auburn University at Montgomery
P.O. Box 244023
Montgomery 36124-4023
334-244-3285; Fax: 334-244-3762

Bessemer State Technical College
P.O. Box 308
Bessemer 35021-0308
205-428-6391; Fax: 205-424-5119

Enterprise State Junior College
P.O. Box 1300
Enterprise 36331-1300
334-347-2623

Jefferson State Community College
2601 Carson Rd.
Birmingham 35215-3098
205-853-1200; Fax: 205-853-0340

John C. Calhoun State Community College
P.O. Box 2216
Decatur 35609-2216
205-306-2500; Fax: 256-306-2885

University of Alabama
P.O. Box 870132, Room 152
Tuscaloosa 35487
205-348-5666; Fax: 205-348-9046

University of Montevello
Station 6030
Montevello 35115
800-292-4349; Fax: 205-665-6030

ARIZONA

Eastern Arizona College
Thatcher 85552-0769
520-428-8251; Fax: 520-428-8462

Glendale Community College
6000 W. Olive
Glendale 85302-3090
602-435-3305; Fax: 602-435-3329

Northern Arizona University
P.O. Box 4084
Flagstaff 86011
520-523-9011; Fax: 520-523-7331

University of Arizona
1110 East South Campus Drive (FCR
Building)
Tucson 85721-0033
520-621-2211; Fax: 520-621-3209

ARKANSAS
Southern Arkansas University
P.O. Box 9382
Magnolia 71753-5000
870-235-4040; Fax: 870-235-4931

CALIFORNIA
American River College
4700 College Oaks Drive
Sacramento 95841-4286
916-484-8171

Cabrillo College
6500 Foquel Dr.
Aptos 95003-3194
408-479-6201

California State University
5151 State University Drive
Los Angeles 90032
213-343-3901

California State University, Northridge
18111 Nordhoff Street
Northridge 91330
818-885-3700

Chabot College
25555 Hesperian Blvd.
Hayward 94545-5001
510-786-6714

College of the Desert
43500 Monterrey Avenue
Palm Desert 92260
760-346-8041; Fax: 760-776-0126

College of Marin
835 College Ave.
Kentfield 94904
415-485-9417

College of San Mateo
3401 CSM Dr.
San Mateo 94402-3784
415-574-6594

DeVry Institute of Technology
901 Corporate Center Drive
Pomona 91768
909-622-9800

Diablo Valley College
321 Golf Club Road
Pleasant Hill 94523
925-685-1230; Fax: 925-685-1551

Fashion Institute of Design and
Merchandising
Costa Mesa Campus
3420 Bristol, Ste. 400
Costa Mesa 92626
714-565-2800

Fashion Institute of Design and
Merchandising
Los Angeles Campus
919 South Grand Avenue
Los Angeles 90015-1421
213-624-120

Fashion Institute of Design and
Merchandising
San Diego Campus
1010 Second Avenue, Suite 200
San Diego 92101
619-235-4515

Fashion Institute of Design and
Merchandising
San Francisco Campus
55 Stockton Street
San Francisco 94108-5829
415-433-6691

Golden West College
15744 Golden West St.
P.O. Box 2748
Huntington Beach 92647-2748
714-895-8121

Grossmont College
8800 Grossmont College Drive
El Cajon 92020
619-465-1700; Fax: 619-644-7922

John F. Kennedy University
12 Altarinda Road
Orinda 94563
510-253-2213

Long Beach City College
4901 East Parsons Street
Long Beach 90808
562-938-4111

Orange Coast College
2701 Fairview Road
Costa Mesa 92628
714-432-5772

Saddleback College
28000 Marguerite Parkway
Mission Viejo 92692
949-582-4500; Fax: 949-347-2431

San Francisco State University
1600 Holloway Avenue
San Francisco 94132
415-338-6486; Fax: 415-338-3880

Santa Clara University
500 El Camino Real
Santa Clara 95053
408-554-4700; Fax: 408-554-5255

Shasta College
P.O. Box 496006
Redding 96043
530-225-4841; Fax: 530-225-4995

Thomas Aquinas College
10000 North Ojai Road
Santa Paula 93060
800-634-9797; Fax: 805-525-0620

University of West Los Angeles
1155 West Arbor Vitae Street
Inglewood 90301-2902
310-215-3339; Fax: 310-313-2124

West Los Angeles College
4800 Freshman Drive
Culver City 90230-3500
310-287-4246; Fax: 310-841-0396

COLORADO

Arapahoe Community College
2500 West College Drive
Littleton 80160-9002
303-794-1550; Fax: 303-797-5935

Colorado Mountain College, Alpine
Campus
P.O. Box 1001
Steamboat Springs 81602
970-870-4417 / 800-621-8559

Colorado State University
Design Merchandising and Consumer
Science
150 Aylesworth Southeast
Fort Collins 80523-1575
970-491-1101; Fax: 970-491-4855

Parks College
9065 Grant St.
Denver 80229-4339
303-457-2757

University of Colorado at Boulder
Campus Box 30
Boulder 80309
303-492-6301

University of Colorado at Colorado
Springs
P.O. Box 7150
Colorado Springs 80933-7150
719-593-3383 / 800-990-8227

CONNECTICUT
Briarwood College
2279 Mount Vernon Rd.
Southington 06489-1057
860-628-4751; Fax: 860-628-6444

Gateway Community-Technical College
60 Sargent Drive
New Haven 06511-5918
203-789-7043

Three Rivers Community-Technical
College
Mahan Drive
Norwich 06360
860-886-1931; Fax: 860-886-0691

University of Bridgeport
380 University Avenue
Bridgeport 06601
203-576-4000; Fax: 203-576-4941

DELAWARE
Delaware Technical & Community
College
Jack F. Owens Campus
Georgetown 19947
302-856-5400; Fax: 302-856-9461

Wesley College
120 North State Street
Dover 19901
302-736-2300; Fax: 302-736-2301

FLORIDA
Florida Atlantic University
777 Glades Road
P.O. Box 3091
Boca Raton 33431-0991
407-367-3040

Florida Community College at
Jacksonville
501 West State Street
Jacksonville 32202-4030
904-632-3110

Florida International University
University Park
Miami 33199
305-348-2363

Florida State University
600 West College Avenue
Tallahassee 32306
850-644-2525

Indian River Community College
3209 Virginia Ave.
Fort Pierce 34981-5599
561-462-4740

International Fine Arts
1737 North Bayshore Drive
Miami 33132
305-373-4684; Fax: 305-374-7946

Palm Beach Community College
4200 Congress Avenue
Lake Worth 3346-4796
561-439-8132; Fax: 561-434-5009

University of Florida
P.O. Box 114000
Gainesville 32611
352-392-1365

University of South Florida
4202 East Fowler Avenue
Tampa 33620
813-974-3350

Webber College
P.O. Box 96
Babson Park 33827
813-638-1431

GEORGIA

DeKalb College
555 North Indian Creek Drive
Clarkston 30021-2396
404-299-4564; Fax: 404-299-4574

Georgia Southern University
P.O. Box 8024
Statesboro 30460
912-681-5391; Fax: 912-681-0081

Kennesaw State University
100 Chastain Road
Kennesaw 30144-5591
770-423-6300; Fax: 770-423-6541

HAWAII

University of Hawaii-Leeward
Community College
96-045 Ala Ike
Pearl City 96782-3366
808-455-0217; Fax: 808-455-0471

IDAHO

College of Southern Idaho
P.O. Box 1238
Twin Falls 83303-1238
208-733-9554; Fax: 208-736

Idaho State University
P.O. Box 8054
Pocatello 83209
208-236-3277

Lewis-Clark State College
500 8th Ave.
Lewiston 83501-2698
208-799-2210; Fax: 208-799-2831

ILLINOIS

Belleville Area College
2500 Carlyle Avenue
Belleville 62221
618-235-2700; Fax: 618-235-1578

Black Hawk College Quad
Cities Campus
6600 34th Avenue
Moline 61265
309-796-1311; Fax: 309-792-5976

Chicago State University
95th Street at King Drive
Chicago 60628
312-995-2513

City Colleges of Chicago, Harold
Washington College
30 East Lake Street
Chicago 60601-2449
312-553-6006; Fax: 312-553-6077

College of Lake County
19351 West Washington St.
Grayslake 60030-1198
847-223-6601

Elgin Community College
1700 Spartan Dr.
Elgin 60123-7193
847-888-7385

Governors State University
Stuenkel Rd.
University Park 60466
708-534-4500; Fax: 708-534-5458

Illinois State University
2200 Admissions
Normal 61761-2200
309-438-2181

John A. Logan College
700 Logan College Rd.
Carterville 62918-9900
618-985-3741; Fax: 618-985-2248

Kankakee Community College
P.O. Box 888
Kankakee 60901
815-933-0242; Fax: 815-933-0217

Lake Land College
5001 Lake Land Blvd.
Mattoon 61938
217-234-5254

MacCormac College
506 South Wabash Avenue
Chicago 60605-1667
630-341-1200; Fax: 630-941-0937

McHenry County College
8900 U.S. Highway 14
Chicago 60012-2761
815-455-3700; Fax: 815-455-8589

Parkland College
2400 West Bradley Avenue
Champaign 61821
217-351-2200; Fax: 217-353-2632

Rock Valley College
3301 North Mulford Road
Rockford 61114
815-654-4250; Fax: 815-654-4254

South Suburban College
15800 South State St.
South Holland 60473-1270
708-596-2000; Fax: 708-210-5710

University of Illinois
506 Wright Street
Urbana 61801
217-333-0302

Waubonsee Community College
Route 47
Sugar Grove 60554-9799
630-466-7900; Fax: 630-466-4964

INDIANA
Ball State University
Business College
Munci 47306
765-289-1241

Indiana University
Apparel Merchandising and Interior
Design
Memorial Hall East, Room 232
Bloomington 47405
812-855-5223; Fax: 812-855-4869

International Business College
3811 Illinois Rd.
Fort Wayne 46804-1217
219-459-4555

Purdue University
Schleman Hall
West Lafayette 47907
765-494-8296

IOWA
American Institute of Business
2500 Fleur Drive
Des Moines 50321-1799
515-244-4221; Fax: 515-244-6773

American Institute of Commerce
1801 East Kimberly Rd.
Davenport 52807-2095
319-355-3500

Des Moines Area Community College
2006 South Ankeny
Ankeny 50021-8995
515-964-6210

Ellsworth Community College
1100 College Ave.
Iowa Falls 50126-1199
515-648-4611; Fax: 515-648-3128

Hawkeye Institute of Technology
1501 East Orange Road
Waterloo 50701
319-296-2320; Fax: 319-296-2874

Iowa Central Community College-Fort
Dodge
330 Avenue M
Fort Dodge 50501
515-576-7201; Fax: 515-576-7206

Iowa Lakes Community College
300 South 18th St.
Estherville 51334-22985
712-362-2604; Fax: 712-362-2260

Iowa State University
314 Alumni Hall
Ames 50011-2010
515-294-5836

Iowa Western Community College
2700 College Rd.
Council Bluffs 51503
712-325-3288; Fax: 712-325-3720

Kirkwood Community College
P.O. Box 2068
221 Lynn Hall
Cedar Rapids 52406-2068
319-398-5517; Fax: 319-398-1244

North Iowa Area Community College
500 College Drive
Mason City 50401
515-423-1264; Fax: 515-423-1711

Northwest Iowa Community College
603 West Park Street
Sheldon 51201-1046
712-324-5061; Fax: 712-324-4136

Southwestern Community College,
Iowa
1501 West Townline Rd.
Creston 50801
515-782-7081; Fax 515-782-3312

University of Northern Iowa
1222 West 27th Street
Cedar Falls 50614-0033
319-273-2281

KANSAS
Allen County Community College
1801 North Cottonwood
Iola 66749-1607
316-365-5116; Fax: 316-365-3284

Butler County Community College,
Kansas
901 South Haverhill
El Dorado 67042-3280
316-321-2222

Coffeyville Community College
400 West 11th St.
Coffeyville 67337-5063
316-251-7700

Cowley County Community College and
Vocational-Technical School
125 South Second
P.O. Box 1147
Arkansas City 67005-2662
316-441-5312; Fax: 316-441-5350

Fort Scott Community College
2108 South Horton
Fort Scott 66701
316-223-2700

Garden City Community College
801 Campus Dr.
Garden City 67846-6399
316-276-7611

Hutchinson Community College and
Area Vocational School
1300 North Plum
Hutchinson 67501-5894
316-665-3536

Kansas State University
119 Anderson Hall
Manhattan 66506
913-532-6250

KENTUCKY
Eastern Kentucky University
521 Lancaster Avenue
Richmond 40475-3101
606-622-2106

University of Kentucky
College of Human Environmental
Sciences
102 Erikson Hall
Lexington 40506-0050
606-257-2878; Fax: 606-257-4095

University of Kentucky, Madisonville
Community College
2000 College Dr.
Madisonville 42431-9185
502-821-2250

University of Kentucky, Maysville
Community College
1755 U.S. 68
Maysville 41056
606-759-7141

University of Kentucky, Paducah
Community College
P.O. Box 7380
Paducah 42002-7380
502-554-9200

Western Kentucky University
1 Big Red Way
Bowling Green 14101
502-745-2551; Fax: 502-745-6133

LOUISIANA
Louisiana State University
School of Human Ecology
Baton Rouge 70803
504-388-2281; Fax:504-388-2697

Louisiana Tech University
P.O. Box 3178
Ruston 71272
318-257-3036; Fax: 318-257-2499

MAINE
Thomas College
180 West River Road
Waterville 04901
207-873-0771; Fax: 207-877-0114

MARYLAND
Allegany Community College of
Maryland
12401 Willowbrook Road Southeast
Cumberland 21502
301-724-7700

Anne Arundel Community College
101 College Parkway
Arnold 21012-1895
410-541-2240

Charles County Community College
910 Mitchell Road
La Plata 20646
301-870-3008; Fax: 301-934-7698

Harford Community College
401 Thomas Run Road
Bell Air 21015
410-836-4000; Fax: 410-836-4265

Hood College
401 Rosemont Avenue
Frederick 21740
800-922-1599; Fax: 301-694-7653

Howard Community College
10901 Little Patuxent Parkway
Columbia 21044-3197
410-992-4856

University of Maryland-Eastern Shore
Princess Anne 21853
410-651-6410

MASSACHUSETTS
Aquinas College at Milton
303 Adams Street
Milton 02186
617-696-3100; Fax: 617-696-8706

Bay State College
122 Commonwealth
Boston 02116
617-236-8000; Fax: 617-536-1735

Bristol Community College
777 Elsbree Street
Fall River 02720
508-678-2811; Fax:508-676-7146

Bunker Hill Community College
250 New Rutherford Avenue
Boston 02129
617-228-2238; Fax: 617-241-5535

Cape Cod Community College
2240 Iyanough Road
West Barnstable 02668
508-362-2131; Fax: 508-375-4020

Dean Junior College
99 Main Street
Franklin 02038
508-528-9100; Fax: 508-541-1922

Endicott College
376 Hale Street
Beverly 01915
978-921-1000; Fax: 978-927-0084

Framingham State College
100 State Street
Framingham 01701
508-626-4500

Holyoke Community College
303 Homestead Avenue
Holyoke 01040-1099
413-538-7000; Fax: 413-534-8975

Lasell College
1844 Commonwealth Avenue
Newton 02160
617-243-2000; Fax: 617-243-2326

Middlesex Community College
33 Kearney Square
Lowell 01852
508-656-3211; Fax: 508-441-1749

Mount Ida College
777 Dedham Street
Newton Centre 02519
617-928-4535

Newbury College
129 Fisher Avenue
Brookline 02445
617-739-0510; Fax: 617-731-9618

Northeastern University
360 Huntington Avenue
Boston 02115
617-373-2200; Fax: 617-373-4804

Roxbury Community College
1234 Columbus Avenue
Roxbury Crossing 02120-3400
617-541-5310

Salem State College
352 Lafayette Street
Salem 01970
508-741-6200

Simmons College
300 The Fenway
Boston 02115
617-521-2051

University of Massachusetts-Amherst
P.O. Box 30120
Amherst 01003
413-545-0222

MICHIGAN
Alma College
614 West Superior St.
Alma 48801-1599
517-463-7139 / 800-321-2562

Baker College of Flint
1050 West Bristol Road
Flint 48507-5508
810-766-4015 / 800-822-2537

Baker College of Muskegon
123 East Apple Avenue
Muskegon 49442-3497
616-726-4904; Fax: 616-728-1417

Baker College of Owosso
1020 South Washington St.
Owosso 48867-4400
517-723-5251

Central Michigan University
102 Warriner
Mt. Pleasant 48859
517-774-3076

Davenport College
415 East Fulton
Grand Rapids 49503
616-451-3511; Fax: 616-732-1185

Delta College
1961 Delta Road
University Center 48710
517-686-9000; Fax: 517-686-8736

Ferris State University
420 Oak St.
Big Rapids 49307
616-592-2100; Fax: 616-592-2978

Lansing Community College
P.O. Box 40010
Lansing 48901-7210
517-483-1252; Fax: 517-483-9668

Michigan State University
250 Administration Bldg.
East Lansing 48824
517-355-8332; Fax: 517-353-1647

Northern Michigan University
1401 Presque Isle Ave.
Marquette 49855-5301
906-227-2650; Fax: 906-227-2204

Northwood Institute
3225 Cook Road
Midland 48640
517-837-4200

Oakland Community College
2480 Opdyke Rd.
Bloomfield Hills 48304-2266
248-540-1500

West Shore Community College
P.O. Box 277
Scottville 49454-0277
616-845-6211; Fax: 616-845-0207

Western Michigan University
West Michigan Ave.
Kalamazoo 49008
616-387-3444

MINNESOTA

University of Minnesota, Crookston
2900 University Ave.
Crookston 56716-5001
218-281-6510; Fax: 218-281-8050

North Hennepin Community College
7411 85th Ave. North
Brooklyn Park 55445-2299
612-424-0713

Northland Community and Technical
College
1101 Highway 1 East
Thief River Falls 56701
218-681-0862; Fax: 218-681-6405

Red Wing/Winona Technical College
P.O. Box 409
Winona 55987
507-453-2732; Fax: 507-453-2715

Ridgewater College
P.O. Box 1097
Willmar 56201-1097
320-231-2902; Fax: 320-231-7677

St. Cloud Technical College
1540 Northway Dr.
St. Cloud 56303-1240
320-654-5089; Fax: 320-654-5981

Winona State University
P.O. Box 5838
Winona 55987-5838
507-457-5100; Fax: 507-457-5586

MISSISSIPPI
Delta State University
Kethley Rm. 105
Cleveland 38733
601-846-4018

Mississippi College
P.O. Box 4203
Clinton, MS 39058-3804
601-925-3240

Southern Mississippi University
P.O. Box 5166
Hattiesburg 39406
601-266-5000

University of Missisippi
University 38677
601-232-7226; Fax: 601-232-5821

MISSOURI
Fontbonne College
6800 Wydown Blvd.
St. Louis 63105
314-889-1400; Fax: 314-889-1451

Jefferson College
1000 Viking Dr.
Hillsboro 63050
314-789-3951; Fax: 314-789-5103

Northwest Missouri State University
800 University Dr.
Maryville 64468
800-633-1175

Southeast Missouri State University
One University Plaza
Cape Girardeau 63701
314-651-2250

University of Missouri-Columbia
230 Jesse Hall
Columbia 65211
573-882-2456

Stephens College
1200 East Broadway
Columbia 65215
314-876-7207

MONTANA
Miles Community College
2715 Dickinson St.
Miles City 59301-4799
406-233-3513; Fax: 406-233-3599

NEBRASKA
Grand Island College
P.O. Box 393
Grand Island 68802-0399
308-382-8044; Fax: 308-382-5072

Southeast Community College, Lincoln
Campus
8800 O St.
Lincoln 68520-1299
402-497-2600

University of Nebraska-Lincoln Campus
14th and R Streets
Lincoln 68588
402-554-2351

NEVADA
Community College of Southern
Nevada
3200 E. Cheyenne Ave.
North Las Vegas 89030-4296
702-651-4060

NEW HAMPSHIRE
Hesser College
3 Sundial Avenue
Manchester 03103-7245
603-668-6660

New Hampshire College
2500 N. River Rd.
Manchester 03106
603-668-2211

NEW JERSEY
Atlantic Community College
5100 Black Horse Pike
Mays Landing 08330-2699
609-343-5000 / 800-645-CHEF

Berkeley College
44 Rifle Camp Road
West Paterson 07424-3353
800-446-5400; Fax: 973-278-2242

Bergen Community College
400 Paramus Road
Paramus 07652
201-447-7100; Fax: 201-670-7973

Camden County College
P.O. Box 200
College Drive
Blackwood 08012
609-227-7200; Fax: 609-374-4856

County College of Morris
214 Center Grove Road
Randolph 07869
973-328-5100; Fax: 973-328-5676

Glouster County College
1400 Tanyard Road
Sewell 08080
609-468-5000; Fax: 609-468-8498

Jersey City State College
2039 Kennedy Boulevard
Jersey City 07305
201-200-3234; Fax: 201-200-2044

Middlesex County College
2600 Woodbridge Avenue
P.O. Box 3050
Edison 08818-3050
732-548-6000; Fax: 732-906-4165

Montclair State University
1 Normal Ave.
Upper Montclair 07043
973-655-5116 / 800-331-9205; Fax:
973-893-5455

Ocean County College
P.O. Box 2001
Toms River 08754-2001
732-255-0304

Raritan Valley Community College
P.O. Box 3300
Somerville 08876
908-526-1200; Fax: 908-429-0268

Rider University
2083 Lawrenceville Rd.
Lawrenceville 08648-3001
609-896-5042; Fax: 609-895-6645

Salem Community College
460 Hollywood Ave.
Carneys Point 08069-2799
609-351-2696

Sussex County Community College
1 College Hill
Newton 07860
973-300-2100

NEW MEXICO
Clovis Community College
417 Schepps Boulevard
Clovis 88101
505-769-2811; Fax: 505-769-4190

Dona Ana Branch Community College
Box 3001
Las Cruces 88003-8001
505-527-7532

NEW YORK

Bernard Baruch College
17 Lexington Avenue
New York 10010
212-802-2300

Berkeley College
3 East 43rd Street
New York 10017-4604
212-986-4343; Fax: 212-697-3371

Berkeley College
40 W. Red Oak Lane
White Plains 10604
914-694-1122 / 800-446-5400; Fax:
914-694-5832

Bryant and Stratton Business Institute
1259 Central Ave.
Albany 12205-5230
518-437-1802 / 888-516-9675; Fax:
518-437-1048

Bryant and Stratton Business Institute
1214 Abbott Rd.
Lackawanna 14218-1989
716-821-9331 / 888-516-9675; Fax:
716-821-9343

Bryant and Stratton Business Institute
8687 Carling Rd.
Liverpool 13090-1315
315-652-6500 / 888-516-9675; Fax:
315-652-5500

Bryant and Stratton Business Institute
82 St. Paul St.
Rochester 14623-1381
716-325-6010 / 888-516-9675; Fax:
716-325-6805

Bryant and Stratton Business Institute
953 James Street
Syracuse 13203-2502
315-472-6603 / 888-516-9675; Fax
474-4383

Bryant and Stratton Business Institute
Eastern Hills Campus
200 Bryant & Stratton Way
P.O. Box 142
Williamsville 14231
716-631-0260 / 888-516-9675; Fax:
716-631-0273

Cazenovia College
220 South Warren St.
Cazenovia 13035
315-655-8005; Fax: 315-655-2190

Central City Business Institute
224 Harrison St.
Syracuse 13202-3052
315-472-6233 / 800-945-CCBI

Clinton Community College
136 Clinton Point Dr.
Plattsburgh 12901-9573
518-562-4120

CUNY, Bronx Community College
W. 181st and University Ave.
Bronx 10453
718-289-5888

CUNY, Kingsborough Community
College
2001 Oriental Boulevard
Brooklyn 11235
718-368-5000

Fashion Institute of Technology
Seventh Avenue at 27th Street
New York 10001-5992
212-217-7999

Jefferson Community College
Coffeen St.
Watertown 13601
315-786-2408

Laboratory Institute of Merchandising
12 East 53rd Street
New York 10022
800-677-1323 / 212-752-1530

New York University
22 Washington Square North
New York 10012-1019
212-998-4515; Fax: 212-995-4902

North Country Community College
P.O. Box 89
Saranac Lake 12983-2046
518-891-2915; Fax: 518-891-2915

Orange County Community College
115 South St.
Middletown 10940-6437
914-341-4030

Russel Sage College
51 First Street
Troy 12180
800 999-3RSC

Sullivan County Community College
1000 LeRoy Rd.
Loch Sheldrake 12759-5151
914-434-5750; Fax: 914-434-4806

SUNY, College of Technology at Alfred
Alfred 14802
607-587-4215; Fax: 607-587-4299

SUNY, Cayuga County Community
College
197 Franklin Street
Auburn 13021
315-255-1743; Fax: 315-255-2117

SUNY, College of Technology at Canton
Cornell Drive
Canton 13617
315-386-7123; Fax: 315-386-7933

SUNY, Community College of the Finger
Lakes
4355 Lakeshore Drive
Canandaigua 14424
716-394-3500; Fax: 716-394-5005

SUNY, Dutchess Community College
53 Pendell Road
Poughkeepsie 12601
914-431-8000

SUNY, Geneseo Community College
1 College Circle
Geneseo 14454
716-245-5571

SUNY, Jamestown Community College
525 Falconer Street
Jamestown 14702
716-665-5220

SUNY, Mohawk Valley Community
College
1101 Sherman Drive
Utica 13501-5394
315-792-5400

SUNY, Monroe Community College
1000 East Henrietta Road
Rochester 14623
716-292-2000

SUNY, Nassau Community College
1 Education Dr.
Garden City 11530-6793
516-572-7210

SUNY, Niagara Community College
3111 Saunders Settlement Road
Sanborn 14132
716-731-3271

SUNY, North County Community
College
20 Winona Avenue
Saranac Lake 12983
518-891-2915

SUNY, Orange County Community
College
115 South Street
Middletown 10940
914-344-6222

SUNY, Suffolk County Community
College
Ammerman Campus
533 College Rd.
Seldon 11784-2851
516-451-4022

SUNY, Sullivan County Community
College
1000 Leroy Road
Loch Sheldrake 12759
914-434-5750; Fax: 914-434-4806

SUNY, Tompkins/Cortland Community
College
170 North Street
P.O. Box 139
Dryden 13053
607-844-8211

SUNY, Ulster County Community
College
Stone Ridge 12484
914-687-5022

Syracuse University
201 Administration Building
Syracuse 13244
315-443-3611

NORTH CAROLINA
Central Piedmont Community College
P.O. Box 35009
Charlotte 28235-5009
704-330-6006

East Carolina University
East 5th Street
Greenville 27858
919-328-6131; Fax: 919-328-6664

Lenoir Community College
P.O. Box 188
Kingston 28502-0188
252-527-6223; Fax: 252-527-1189

Surry Community College
P.O. Box 304
Dobson 27017
336-386-8121; Fax: 336-386-8951

University of North Carolina-Greensboro
1000 Spring Garden St.
Greensboro 27402
336-334-5000

NORTH DAKOTA
Bismark State College
P.O. Box 5587
Bismark 58506-5587
701-224-5400; Fax: 701-224-5550

Minot State University-Bottineau
105 Simrall
Bottineau 58318-1198
701-228-5426

North Dakota State University
Department of Apparel Textiles and
Interior Design
1301 N. 12th St.
Fargo, North Dakota 58105
701-231-8223

University of North Dakota-Grand Forks
P.O. Box 8098
Grand Forks 58202
701-777-3304; Fax: 701-777-5099

OHIO
Bluffton College
280 West College Avenue
Bluffton 45817
800-488-3257

Bowling Green State University
110 McFall Center
Bowling Green 43403
419-372-2086

Bowling Green State University-
Firelands College
1 University Dr.
Huron 44839-9791
419-433-5560

Bryant and Stratton College, Parma
12955 Snow Rd.
Parma 44130-1013
216-265-3151; Fax: 216-265-0325

Columbus State Community College
107 North 9th Street
Columbus 43215-3875
614-227-2400; Fax: 614-227-5117

Dyke College
112 Prospect Avenue
Cleveland 44115-1096
216-696-9000

Miami-Jacobs Junior College of
Business
400 East Second Street
Dayton 45402
937-461-5174; Fax: 937-461-3384

Edison State Community College
1973 Edison Dr.
Piqua 45356-9253
937-778-8600; Fax: 937-778-1920

Hocking College
3301 Hocking Pkwy.
Nelsonville 45764-9588
740-753-3591

Jefferson Community College
4000 Sunset Blvd.
Steubenville 43952-3595
740-264-5591; Fax: 740-264-1338

Lima Technical College
4240 Campus Drive
Lima 45804-3597
419-995-8000; Fax: 419-995-8098

Lorain County Community College
1005 N. Abbe Rd.
Elyria 44035
440-365-4191; Fax: 440-365-6519

Miami University
500 E. High St.
Oxford 45056
513-529-1809

Northwest State Community College
22-600 State Route 34
Archbold 43502
419-267-5511; Fax: 419-267-5692

Ohio University
120 Chubb Hall
Athens 45701-2979
740-593-2880

Ohio University-Eastern
45425 National Rd.
St. Clairsville 43950-9724
740-695-1720

University of Rio Grande
218 N. College Ave.
Rio Grande 45674-3131
740-245-5353

University of Toledo
2801 West Bancroft Street
Toledo 43606
419-537-4242

Wright State University, Lake Campus
7600 State Route 703
Celina 45822-2921
419-586-0324; Fax: 419-586-0358

Youngstown State University
410 Wick Ave.
Youngstown 44555-0002
216-742-3150; Fax: 216-742-1998

OKLAHOMA

Southeastern Oklahoma State
University
P.O. Box 4139
Durant 74701-0609
580-924-0121

University of Central Oklahoma
100 North University
Edmond 73034
405-341-2980; Fax: 405-330-3821

Western Oklahoma State College
2801 N. Main
Altus 73521-1397
580-477-2000; Fax: 580-521-6154

OREGON

Bassist College
2000 Southwest Fifth Ave.
Portland 97207
503-228-6528 / 800-547-0937;
Fax: 503-228-4227

PENNSYLVANIA

Bucks County Community College
434 Swamp Road
Newtown 18940
215-968-8000; Fax: 215-504-8509

Butler County Community College
P.O. Box 1203
Butler 16003
412-287-8711

Cedar Crest College
100 College Drive
Allentown 18104
610-740-3780; Fax: 610-437-5955

Central Pennsylvania Business School
College Hill Rd.
Summerdale 17093-0309
717-732-0702; Fax: 717-732-5254

Community College of Allegheny
County
Allegheny Campus
808 Ridge Avenue
Pittsburgh 15233
412-237-2525

Community College of Allegheny
County
Boyce Campus
595 Beatty Road
Monroeville 15146
412-371-8651; Fax: 724-325-6797

Community College of Allegheny
County
North Campus
8701 Perry Highway
Pittsburgh 15237
412-366-7000; Fax: 412-369-3624

Community College of Philadelphia
1700 Spring Garden Street
Philadelphia 19130-3991
215-972-6361; Fax: 215-972-6361

Delaware County Community College
901 Media Line Rd.
Media 19063-1094
610-359-5333

Drexel University
32nd and Chestnut Streets
Philadelphia 19104
215-895-2400

Harcum College
750 Montgomery Ave.
Bryn Mawr 19010-3476
610-526-6107; Fax: 610-526-6147

Harrisburg Area Community College
1 HACC Drive
Harrisburg 17110-2999
717-780-2406; Fax: 717-231-7674

La Salle University
1900 W. Olney Ave.
Philadelphia 19141-1199
215-951-1500 / 800-382-1910; Fax:
215-951-1488

Marywood College
2300 Adams Avenue
Scranton 18509-1598
717-348-6234 / 800-346-5014

Newport Business Institute
945 Greensburg Rd.
Lower Burrell 15068-3929
724-339-7542 / 800-752-7695; Fax:
724-339-7542

Philadelphia College of Textiles and
Science
School House Lane and Henry Avenue
Philadelphia 19144
215-951-2800

Pennsylvania College of Technology
1 College Avenue
Williamsport 17701
717-327-4761; Fax: 717-327-4529

Reading Area Community College
P.O. Box 1706
Reading 19603-1706
610-372-4271; Fax: 610-375-8255

Saint Vincent College
300 Fraser Purchase Road
Latrobe 15650-2690
724-537-4540; Fax: 724-537-4554

Seton Hill College
Seton Hill Dr.
Greensburg 15601-1599
724-838-4255

The Art Institute of Pittsburgh
526 Penn Avenue
Pittsburgh 15222-3269
412-263-6600

Westmoreland County Community
College
Youngwood 15697
724-925-4060; Fax: 724-925-1150

York College of Pennsylvania
York 17405-7199
717-846-7788

RHODE ISLAND
Community College of Rhode Island
Knight/Flanagan Campus
400 East Ave.
Warwick 02886-1807
401-825-2285; Fax: 401-825-2418

Johnson & Whales University
8 Abbott Park Place
Providence 02903
800-343-2565

SOUTH CAROLINA
Spartanburg Technical College
P.O. Box 4386
Spartanburg 29305-4386
864-591-3800

University of South Carolina
Columbia 29208
803-777-7700

SOUTH DAKOTA
South Dakota State
P.O. Box 2201
Brooking 57007
800-952-3541; Fax: 605-688-6386

TENNESSEE
Belmont College
1900 Belmont Boulevard
Nashville 37212-3757
615-385-6785

Chattanooga State Technical
Community College
4501 Amnicola Highway
Chattanooga 37406-1018
423-697-4404; Fax: 423-478-6255

University of Tennessee
615 McCallie Avenue
Chattanooga 37403
423-974-1000

University of Tennessee, Knoxville
320 Student Services Building
Knoxville 37996-0230
615-974-2184

TEXAS
Austin Community College
5930 Middle Fiskville Road
Austin 78752-4390
512-223-7000; Fax: 512-223-7791

Baylor University
P.O. Box 97056
Waco 76798
254-710-3435 / 800-BAYLOR U;
Fax: 254-710-1092

Brookhaven College
3939 Valley View Lane
Farmers Branch 75244-4997
972-860-4604; Fax: 972-860-4897

Central Texas College
P.O. Box 1800
Killeen 76542-4199
254-526-1104

Cisco Junior College
Rte. 3, Box 3
Cisco 76437-9321
254-442-2567

Del Mar College
Baldwin and Ayres
Corpus Christi 78404-3897
512-886-1248

Midland College
3600 N. Garfield
Midland 79705-6399
915-685-4503

Navarro College
3200 West 7th Ave.
Corsicana 75110-4899
903-874-6501

South Plains College
1401 College Ave.
Levelland 79336-6595
806-894-9611; Fax: 806-894-5274

Stephen F. Austin State University
P.O. Box Admissions 13051
Nacogdoches 75962-3051
409-468-2504; Fax: 409-468-2261

Tarrant County Junior College
1500 Hudson Street
Fort Worth 76102-6599
817-515-7851

Texarkana College
2500 North Robison Road
Texarkana 75599-0001
903-838-4541; Fax: 903-832-5030

Texas A&M University, College Station
217 John J. Koldus Bldg.
College Station 77843-1265
409-845-3741

Texas A&M University, Kingsville
Campus Box 105
Kingsville 78363
512-593-2111

Texas Southmost College
83 Fort Brown
Brownsville 78520-4991
210-544-8254

Texas Women's University
P.O. Box 22909
Denton 76204
940-898-3040; Fax: 940-898-2120

University of North Texas
Box 13797
Denton 76203-3797
940-565-2000; Fax: 940-565-4640

West Texas A&M University
WT Box 907
Canyon 79016-0001
806-656-2020

UTAH
Brigham Young University
Admissions
A-153 ASB
Provo 84602
801-378-2500

LDS Business College
411 East South Temple Street
Salt Lake City 84111-1392
801-524-8142; Fax: 801-524-1900

Salt Lake Community College
P.O. Box 30808
Salt Lake City 84130-0808
801-957-4297; Fax: 801-957-4522

Utah State University
University Hill
Logan 84322-1600
801-797-1096

Weber State University
1137 University Circle
Ogden 84408-1137
801-626-6743

VERMONT
Champlain College
163 South Willard Street
P.O. Box 670
Burlington 05402-0670
802-860-2727

VIRGINIA
Central Virginia Community College
3506 Wards Rd.
Lynchburg 24502-4907
804-832-7600

Christopher Newport University
50 Shoe Lane
Newport News 23606-2998
757-594-7015; Fax: 804-594-7713

Commonwealth College, Hampton
1120 West Mercury Boulevard
Hampton 23666-3309
757-838-2122; Fax: 757-499-7799

Commonwealth College, Virginia Beach
301 Centre Pointe Drive
Virginia Beach 23462-4417
757-499-7900; Fax: 757-499-7799

James Madison University
800 S. Main St.
Harrisonburg 22807
540-568-6147

Marymount University
2807 North Glebe Road
Arlington 22207-4299
703-284-1500; Fax: 703-527-3830

Norfolk State University
2401 Corprew Avenue
Norfolk 23504
757-683-8396

Virginia Commonwealth University
901 West Franklin Street
Richmond 23284-9005
804-828-1222

Virginia Tech University
104 Burruss Hall
Blacksburg 24061-0202
540-231-6267; Fax: 540-231-3242

WASHINGTON

Central Washington University
400 E. 8th Ave.
Ellensburg 98926
509-963-3001; Fax: 509-963-3022

Centralia College
600 W. Locust
Centralia 98531-4099
360-736-9391

Clark College
1800 E. McLoughlin Blvd.
Vancouver 98663-3598
360-992-2107

Edmonds Community College
20,000 68th Ave. West
Lynnwood 98036-5999
425-640-1416; Fax: 425-771-3366

Everett Community College
801 Westmore Avenue
Everett 98201-1327
425-388-9219

Green River Community College
12401 Southeast 320th Street
Auburn 98092-3699
253-833-9111; Fax: 253-939-5135

Shoreline Community College
16101 Greenwood Ave. North
Seattle 98133-5696
206-546-4581; Fax: 206-546-5835

Skagit Valley College
2405 E. College Way
Mount Vernon 98273-5899
360-416-7620

Spokane Falls Community College
3410 West Fort Wright Drive
Spokane 99224
509-533-3500

Walla Walla Community College
500 Tausick Way
Walla Walla 99362-9267
509-527-4283; Fax: 509-527-3361

WEST VIRGINIA

Fairmont State College
1201 Locust Ave.
Fairmont 26554
304-367-4141

Marshall University
400 Hal Greer Boulevard
Huntington 25755
304-696-3160; Fax: 304-696-4344

Shepherd College
Shepherdstown 25433
304-876-5212 / 800-344-5231;
Fax: 304-876-3101

West Liberty State College
P.O. Box 295
West Liberty 26074
304-336-8076; Fax: 304-336-8285

WISCONSIN

Fox Valley Technical College
1825 N. Bluemound Dr.
P.O. Box 2277
Appleton 54913-2277
920-735-5713; Fax: 920-735-2582

Milwaukee Area Technical College
700 West State Street
Milwaukee 53233
414-297-6600; Fax: 414-297-7689

University of Wisconsin at Madison
750 University Avenue
Madison 53706
608-262-0471; Fax: 608-265-6041

University of Wisconsin-Stout Campus
P.O. Box 790
Menomonie 54751
715-232-1431

Western Wisconsin Technical College
La Crosse Campus
P.O. Box C908
La Crosse 54602
800-248-9982; Fax: 608-785-9202

WYOMING
Casper College
125 College Dr.
Casper 82601-4699
307-268-2491

Central Wyoming College
2660 Peck Avenue
Riverton 82501-2092
307-855-2231; Fax: 307-855-2092

Laramie County Community College
1400 E. College Dr.
Cheyenne 82007-3299
307-778-5222; Fax: 307-778-1399

Northwest College
231 W. 6th St.
Powell 82435-1898
307-754-6601; Fax: 307-754-6700

A FINAL WORD OF PLANNING YOUR RETAILING EDUCATION

Remember to read chapter two for more information about selecting and planning
to enroll in the school of your choice. Read chapter four on how to take advantage
of financial aid resources to help you pay for your retail education.

THE INSIDE TRACK

Who:	Darin Finkelstein
What:	Divisional Merchandise Manager, Burdines Men's Sportwear and Collection
Where:	Miami, Florida
Education:	Bachelor's degree

Insider's Advice

I work to grow the business from where it was a year ago. I manage four buyers. We try to buy the goods to meet the needs of customers in different regions where the stores are. I interface with my boss and with the vendors/suppliers. I attend fashion shows. I travel to New York, San Francisco, Atlanta, and Las Vegas. I generate and analyze reports. I help in store planning and work on floor plans. I review advertising and markdown decisions, identify buying trends, go to meetings of my staff. I'm on the phone a lot!

To excel quickly in retailing takes a lot. You have to dedicate a lot of time, and you have to have a passion for it. The hours are tough; the systems are challenging to learn; these factors can be frustrating or even overwhelming at first.

Still, the daily "report cards" of how your decisions affect sales provide immediate feedback and motivate you to do better. You're competing against yourself, your peers, and the competition. The results are inspected every day, and everyone in the company can see it. Business is very dynamic and ever-changing. You can make projections, but sometimes it'll surprise you.

Insider's Take on the Future

To develop my career I want to be a divisional merchandise manager in a different area, such as women's apparel or cosmetics. I've been promoted four times in eight years. Then perhaps become a group merchandise manager. I may go for my master's degree later on.

Department stores are too driven by big brands that can be found in many stores. We need to give our customer a unique reason to shop our stores. We're going to need to diversify, offer a broader spectrum of goods.

CHAPTER | 4

This chapter gives you an idea of how much your education will cost (according to what kind of school or training program you choose), what kind of financial aid is available, and where you need to go to find that funding.

FINANCIAL AID FOR THE TRAINING YOU NEED

A college education is expensive: upwards of $100,000 for four years at many private colleges and universities and more than $50,000 for four years even at lower-cost, state-supported colleges. Community and technical colleges are less expensive, but can still run several thousand dollars every semester for tuition, books, lab fees, and other required expenses.

DON'T PANIC: THERE'S HELP AVAILABLE

Figuring out how you and your family will come up with the money to pay for your education requires planning, perseverance, and learning as much as you can about the options available.

If your family has not saved the total amount you will need for college or does not earn enough to cover your expenses, attending college—even the college of your choice—is not a lost cause. Not by any means! That's what financial aid is all about. The amount you and your family will be required to contribute toward your college expenses will be based upon how much you and your family already have and how much you can earn. But if this is not enough, the rest of the expenses can usually be met through financial aid programs.

You can often qualify for some type of financial aid even if you're attending college only part time. The financial aid you'll get may be less than in full-time programs, but it can still be worthwhile and help you pay for a portion of your training program.

Don't let financial aid anxiety deter you from finding out more about the many options you have for financing your training program. Take a deep breath and relax. During the time it takes you to finish this chapter, you can get a handle on the financial aid process. There are, of course, whole books devoted to financial aid, some of which are listed at the end of this chapter; others are listed in Appendix B. Also, most schools have good financial aid advisors, who can address your concerns and help you fill out the necessary paperwork. So there is no shortage of information available to you. Take advantage of it today!

SOME MYTHS ABOUT FINANCIAL AID

There's a lot of confusion out there about financial aid. Here are three of the most common myths that need to be cleared up.

Myth #1: All the red tape involved in finding sources and applying for financial aid is too confusing for me.
Fact: Although you do need to jump through some hoops to get financial aid, it's really not as confusing as you might think. The whole financial aid process is really a set of steps that are ordered and logical. Besides, several sources of help are available to you. For instance, reading this chapter will offer you a helpful overview of the entire process and give you tips on how to get the most financial aid you can. There are also resources at the end of this chapter where you can find additional help. If you believe you'll be able to cope with college, you'll surely be able to cope with looking for the money to go, especially if you take the process one step at a time in an organized manner.

Myth #2: For most students financial aid just means getting a loan and going into heavy debt, which isn't worth it, or working while in school, which will lead to burn-out and poor grades.
Fact: In addition to federal grants and scholarships, most schools have their own grants and scholarships, which the student doesn't have to pay back, and many students get these. It's also possible to get a combination of scholarships and loans.

It's worth taking out a loan if it means attending the school you really want to attend, rather than settling for second choice or not going to school at all. As for working while in school, it's true that it is a challenge to hold down a full-time or even part-time job while in school, but a small amount of work-study employment while attending classes (10-12 hours per week) actually improves academic performance because it teaches students important time-management skills. You can attend a small college or technical school and even a university without paying a dime *if* you know what to do and if you can establish adequate financial need. This chapter will help you apply for the financial aid you need and get you into the program of your choice without emptying your wallet.

Myth #3: I can't understand the financial aid process because of all the unfamiliar terms and strange acronyms that are used.

Fact: While you will come across many acronyms and some unfamiliar terms while applying for federal financial aid, when you refer to the acronym list and glossary at the end of this chapter, you'll find quick definitions and clear explanations of them all.

GETTING STARTED

Complete the Free Application for Federal Student Aid

The first step in beginning the financial aid process is to get the Free Application for Federal Student Aid (FAFSA) form. You can get this form from several sources:

* your public library
* your school's financial aid office
* on-line at www.finaid.org/finaid.html
* calling 1-800-4-FED-AID

You need to get an original form to mail in; photocopies of federal forms are not acceptable. In financial aid circles, this form is commonly referred to by its initials: FAFSA. The FAFSA determines your eligibility status for *all* grants and loans provided by federal or state governments and certain college or institutional aid. Therefore, completeing the FAFSA is the first step in the financial aid process; you should do it as soon as possible.

Many sources of financial aid require students to complete a FAFSA in order to become eligible for financial aid. If you are computer savvy, you can visit a Web site where you fill out and submit the FAFSA on-line. You'll need to print out, sign, and send in the release and signature pages.

The PROFILE Financial Aid Form

Some colleges require applicants seeking financial aid to complete the PROFILE form. The PROFILE Registration is a one-page form. These forms are available in most high school guidance offices or through the College Board's ExPAN application service.

On your PROFILE Registration Form, you must fill in basic demographic information about your family and list all the colleges you've applied to that require the Financial Aid PROFILE. Do not list colleges that don't use it. (Find out if your preferred college requires it early in the process.) You then send this registration form to the College Scholarship Service together with the required payment. You can also call in the information or fax the form, using a credit card to pay the required fee. You can request overnight delivery service for an additional charge if a financial aid deadline is approaching.

A few weeks after you've submitted the completed form (unless you've requested overnight delivery), you'll receive in the mail a customized financial aid application to be used to apply for aid at the colleges you've designated, as well as from certain private scholarship organizations like the National Merit Scholarship program. This form will contain all the questions necessary to estimate your family contribution based on the federal formula plus the specific questions that the colleges and organizations you've designated want answered. Your packet will also contain codes to tell you which colleges want which additional questions and a customized cover letter with information about deadlines and any special requirements for the colleges and programs you designated on the PROFILE Registration. If any of the colleges you're applying to require supplemental forms, such as the Business/Farm Supplement or the Divorced/Separated Parent's Statement, they will be included in the package, too.

Be sure to submit your PROFILE by the earliest deadline given. Two to four weeks after you do, you will receive an acknowledgment and a report that will contain your estimated federal Expected Family Contribution (from your FAFSA) and a second family contribution calculated from the additional data elements you provided. This calculation is called the Institutional Methodology, and colleges that require the PROFILE use this methodology when they award their own funds in conjunction with federal aid.

Remember, if any college you are applying to requires the PROFILE, then you'll have to complete both forms. On the PROFILE, list the colleges you are applying to that require it. On the FAFSA, list all the colleges you are applying to.

Create a Financial Aid Calendar

The second step of beginning the financial aid process is to create a financial aid calendar. You can use any standard calendar—wall, desk, or portable—to do this step. The main thing is to write all of the application deadlines for each step of the financial aid process on one calendar, so you can see at a glance what needs to be done when.

You can start this calendar by writing in the date you request your FAFSA. Then mark down when you receive it and when you send in the completed form. Add important dates and deadlines as you progress though each phase of the financial aid process. Using and maintaining a calendar will help the whole financial aid process run more smoothly and give you peace of mind that the important dates are written down and are not merely bouncing around in your head.

DETERMINING YOUR ELIGIBILITY

To receive federal financial aid from an accredited college or institution's student aid program, you must:

- ◆ Have a high school diploma or its equivalent (GED), pass a test approved by the U.S. Department of Education, or meet other standards your state establishes that are approved by the U.S. Department of Education.
- ◆ Be enrolled or accepted for enrollment as a regular student working toward a degree or certificate in an eligible program.
- ◆ Be a U.S. citizen or eligible non-citizen possessing a social security number. Refer to Immigration and Naturalization Service (INS) in the section entitled Financial Aid Resources that appears at the end of this chapter if you are not a U.S. citizen and are unsure of your eligibility.
- ◆ Make satisfactory academic progress. This means you must stay in good standing with the school, usually defined as maintaining at least a "C" grade average (defined as 2.0 or better on a 4 point scale, in which an "A" is worth 4 points, a "B" is worth 3 points, a "C" is worth 2 points, a "D" worth 1 point, and an "F" or an incomplete worth zero points).
- ◆ Sign a statement of educational purpose and a certification statement on overpayment and default.
- ◆ Register with Selective Services, if required.
- ◆ Have financial need, except for some loan and other aid programs.

You are eligible to apply for federal financial aid by completing the FAFSA even if you haven't yet been accepted or enrolled in a school. However, you do need to be enrolled in an accredited training program in order to actually receive any funds from a federal financial aid program.

WHEN TO APPLY

Apply for financial aid as soon as possible after January 1 of the year in which you plan to enroll in school. For example, if you want to begin school in the fall of 1999, then you should apply for financial aid as soon as possible after January 1, 1999. It is easier to complete the FAFSA after you have completed your tax return, so you may want to consider filing your taxes as early as possible as well.

Do not sign, date, or send your application before January 1 of the year for which you are seeking aid. If you apply by mail, send your completed application in the envelope that came with the original application. The envelope is already addressed, and using it will make sure your application reaches the correct address.

You must reapply for financial aid every year. However, after your first year, you will receive a Student Aid Report (SAR) in the mail before the application deadline. If no corrections need to be made, you can just sign it and send it in.

Many students lose out on thousands of dollars in grants and loans because they file too late. When you fill out the Free Application for Federal Student Aid (FAFSA), you are applying for all aid available, both federal and state, work-study, student loans, etc. The important thing is complying with the deadline date. Those students who do are considered for the Pell Grant, the SEOG (Supplemental Educational Opportunity Grant) and the Perkins Loan, which is the best loan as far as interest goes. Lots of students miss the June 30 deadline, and it can mean losing out on lots of money you can use to help defray education costs. College financial aid officers regret that many students, usually the ones who need the money most, often ignore the deadlines.

After you mail in your completed FAFSA, your application will be processed in approximately four weeks. Then, you will receive a Student Aid Report (SAR) in the mail. The SAR will report the information from your application and, if there are no questions or problems with your application, your SAR will report your Expected Family Contribution (EFC), the number used to determine your eligibility for federal student aid. Each school you list on the application may also receive your application information if the school is set up to receive the information electronically.

Getting Your Forms Filed

Getting your forms filed is as simple as one, two, three.

1. Get an original Federal Application for Federal Student Aid (FAFSA).

Remember to pick up an original copy of this form as photocopies are not acceptable.

2. Fill out the entire FAFSA as completely as possible.

Make an appointment with a financial aid counselor if you need help. Read the forms completely, and don't skip any relevant portions.

3. Return the FAFSA before the deadline date.

Financial aid counselors warn that many students don't file the forms before the deadline and lose out on available aid. Don't be one of those students!

FINANCIAL NEED

Financial aid from many of the programs discussed in this chapter is awarded on the basis of financial need (except for unsubsidized Stafford, PLUS, and Consolidation loans, and some scholarships and grants). When you apply for federal student aid by completing the FAFSA, the information you report is used in a formula established by the U.S. Congress. The formula determines your Expected Family Contribution (EFC), an amount you and your family are expected to contribute toward your education. If your EFC is below a certain amount, you'll be eligible for a federal Pell grant, assuming you meet all other eligibility requirements.

There isn't a maximum EFC that defines eligibility for the other financial aid options. Instead, your EFC is used in an equation to determine your financial needs.

> **Cost of Attendance – EFC = Financial Need**

Your financial aid administrator calculates your cost of attendance and subtracts the amount you and your family are expected to contribute toward that cost. If there's anything left over, you're considered to have financial need.

ARE YOU CONSIDERED DEPENDENT OR INDEPENDENT?

You need to find out if you are defined as a *dependent* or an *independent* student by the federal government. Federal policy uses strict and specific criteria to make this designation, and that criteria applies to all applicants for federal student aid equally.

A dependent student is expected to have parental contribution to school expenses, and an independent student is not. The parental contribution depends on the number of parents with earned income, their income and assets, the age of the older parent, the family size, and the number of family members enrolled in post-secondary education. Income is not just the adjusted gross income from the tax return, but also includes nontaxable income such as social security benefits and child support.

You're an independent student if at least one of the following applies to you:

* you are at least 24 years old
* you're married (even if you're separated)
* you have legal dependents other than a spouse who get more than half of their support from you and will continue to get that support during the award year
* you're an orphan or ward of the court (or were a ward of the court until age 18)
* you're a student seeking a graduate or professional degree
* you're a veteran of the U.S. Armed Forces—formerly engaged in active service in the U.S. Army, Navy, Air Force, Marines, or Coast Guard or as a cadet or midshipman at one of the service academies—released under a condition other than dishonorable. (ROTC students, members of the National Guard, and most reservists are not considered veterans, nor are cadets and midshipmen still enrolled in one of the military service academies.)

If you live with your parents, and if they claimed you as a dependent on their last tax return, then your need will be based on your parents' income. You do not qualify for independent status just because your parents have decided to not claim you as an exemption on their tax return or do not want to provide financial support for your college education.

Students are classified as dependent or independent because federal student aid programs are based on the idea that students (and their parents or spouse, if applicable) have the primary responsibility for paying for their post-secondary, i.e., after high school, education.

GATHERING FINANCIAL RECORDS

Your financial need for most grants and loans depends on your financial situation. Now that you've determined if you are considered a dependent or independent student, you'll know whose financial records you need to gather for this step of the process. If you are a dependent student, then you must gather not only your own financial records, but also those of your parents because you must report their income and assets as well as your own when you complete the FAFSA. If you are an independent student, then you need to gather only your own financial records (and those of your spouse if you're married). Gather your tax records from the year prior to the year for which you are applying. For example, if you apply for the fall of 1998, you will use your tax records from 1997.

To help you fill out the FAFSA, gather the following documents:

* U.S. Income Tax Returns (IRS Form 1040, 1040A, or 1040EZ) for the year that just ended and W-2 and 1099 forms
* records of untaxed income, such as Social Security benefits, AFDC or ADC, child support, welfare, pensions, military subsistence allowances, and veterans' benefits
* current bank statements and mortgage information
* medical and dental expenses for the past year that weren't covered by health insurance
* business and/or farm records
* records of investments such as stocks, bonds, and mutual funds, as well as bank certificates of deposit (CDs) and recent statements from money market accounts
* social security number(s)

Even if you do not complete your federal income tax return until March or April, you should not wait to file your FAFSA until your tax returns are filed with the IRS. Instead, use estimated income information and submit the FAFSA, as noted earlier, just as soon as possible after January 1. Be as accurate as possible, but you can correct estimates later.

TYPES OF FINANCIAL AID

There are many types of financial aid available to help with school expenses. Three general categories exist for financial aid:

1. grants and scholarships—aid that you don't have to pay back
2. work-study—aid that you earn by working
3. loans—aid that you have to pay back

Grants

Grants are a wonderful form of financial aid because they do not need to be paid back. They are normally awarded based on financial need. Here are the two most common forms of grants:

Federal Pell Grants

Federal Pell grants are based on financial need and are awarded only to under-graduate students who have not yet earned a bachelor's or professional degree. For many students, Pell grants provide a foundation of financial aid to which other aid may be added. Awards for each year depend on program funding. The maximum award for the 1996-1997 award year was $2,470. You can receive only one Pell grant in an award year, and you may not receive Pell grant funds for more than one school at a time.

How much you get will depends not only on your Expected Family Contri-bution (EFC) but on your cost of attendance, whether you're a full-time or part-time student, and whether you attend school for a full academic year or less. You can qualify for a Pell grant even if you are only enrolled part-time in a training program. You should also be aware that some private and school-based sources of financial aid will not consider your eligibility if you haven't first applied for a Pell grant.

Federal Supplemental Educational Opportunity Grants (FSEOG)

A Federal Supplemental Educational Opportunity Grant (FSEOG) is for under-graduates with exceptional financial need—that is, students with the lowest Expected Family Contributions (EFCs). It gives priority to students who receive federal Pell grants. Like a Pell grant, it doesn't need to be paid back.

You can receive between $100 and $4,000 a year, depending on when you apply, your level of need, and the funding level of the school you're attending. There's no guarantee that every eligible student will be able to receive a FSEOG. Students at each school are paid based on the availability of funds at that school, and not all schools participate in this program. To have the best chances of getting this grant, apply as early as you can after January 1 of the year in which you plan to attend school.

Scholarships

Scholarships are almost always awarded for academic merit or for special characteristics (for example, ethnic heritage, interests, sports, parent's employer, college major, geographic location, etc.) rather than financial need. You can obtain scholarships from federal, state, school, and private sources.

To find private sources of aid, spend a few hours in the library looking at scholarship and fellowship books, or consider a reasonably priced (under $30) scholarship search service. See the Resources section at the end of this chapter for scholarship book titles and search services contact information. If you're currently employed, check to see if your employer has scholarships or tuition reimbursement programs available. If you're a dependent student, ask your parents, aunts, uncles, and cousins to check with groups or organizations they belong to for possible aid sources. You never know what type of private aid you might dig up. For example, any of the following groups may know of money that could be yours:

- religious organizations
- fraternal organizations
- clubs, such as the Rotary, American Legion, or 4H
- athletic clubs
- veterans' groups
- ethnic group associations
- corporations
- unions

If you have already selected the school you will attend, check with a financial aid administrator (FAA) in the financial aid department to find out if you qualify for any school-based scholarships or other aid. Many schools are offering merit-based scholarships for students with a high school GPA of a certain level or with a certain level of SAT scores in order to attract more students to their school.

While you are looking for sources of scholarships, continue to enhance your chances of winning a scholarship by participating in extracurricular or community events and volunteer activities. You should also obtain references from people who know you well and are leaders in the community, so you can submit their names and/or letters with your scholarship applications.

Make a list of any awards you've received in the past or other honors that you could list on your scholarship application.

Here are a few samples of scholarships that you might be eligible for:

National Merit Scholarships

About 5,000 students each year receive this scholarship, based solely on academic performance in high school, from the National Merit Scholarship Corporation. If you are a high school senior who has excellent grades and who has scored high on tests such as the ACT and SAT, this scholarship may be for you.

The Hope Scholarship

The Hope Scholarship is a Georgia lottery-funded scholarship for students who keep a 3.0 Grade Point Average or higher.

New Hampshire Charitable Fund Student Aid Program

The New Hampshire Charitable Fund Student Aid Program offers scholarships to New Hampshire residents.

J. L. Firmage Marketing Scholarship

This scholarship is one $2,612 award given to an outstanding marketing major with financial need who is pursuing a career in retailing.

May Department Store Foundation

May Department Store Foundation offers two awards of $500 each. One junior and one senior, each with a cumulative 3.2 GPA. If possible, candidates should have an interest in retailing.

J.C. Penney Company Retailing Scholarship

This is $500–$1,000 awarded to a junior or first semester senior. Criteria include: Minimum GPA 3.0, completion of Retail Marketing Strategy (MKT425) or a 3-unit Independent Study (MKT499) focusing on a retail topic before graduation and a summer internship with J.C. Penney. Recognizes a marketing major who is interested in a retail management career.

Military Scholarships

Military scholarships such as the G.I. Bill are available if you are applying to the Army, Navy, Air Force, or Marines, and you may get other money for college or to pay off previous loans.

WORK-STUDY PROGRAMS

A variety of work-study programs exist for students. If you already know what school you want to attend, you can find out about its school-based work-study options from the student employment office. Look especially carefully into the Federal Work-Study (FWS) Program.

The FWS Program provides jobs for undergraduate students with financial need, allowing them to earn money to help pay education expenses. The program encourages community service work and work related to the student's course of study. You'll earn at least minimum wage and maybe more, depending on the type of work and your skills. The amount of the FWS award will depend on the following:

+ when you apply (again, *apply early*)
+ your level of need
+ the funds available at your particular school

As an undergraduate, you'll be paid by the hour (a graduate student may receive a salary), and you will receive the money directly from your school at least monthly you cannot be paid by commission or fee. You'll work either on campus for your school, or off-campus for a private nonprofit organization or public agency engaged in "work in the public interest." Students may earn up to the amount of their award at any time during the award period, as long as they do not work more than 20 hours per week. The awards are not transferable from year to year. Not all schools have work-study programs in every area of study.

If you cannot finance your entire training program through scholarships, grants, or work-study exclusively, the next step is to consider taking out a loan. Be cautious about the amount you borrow, but remember that it may be worth it to borrow money to attend a training program that will enhance your future job prospects.

STUDENT LOANS

The first step in finding a student loan is to learn the basics of loan programs. Become familiar with the various student loan programs, especially with government loans. You can get a good head start on this process by reading the rest of this chapter. To get more detailed information than appears here, seek guidance from a financial aid administrator or banking institution.

Questions to Ask Before You Take out a Loan

In order to get the facts and clearly understand the loan you're about to take out, ask the following questions:

1. *What is the interest rate and how often is the interest capitalized?* Your college's financial aid administrator (FAA) may be able to tell you this.

2. *What fees will be charged?* Government loans generally have an origination fee, which goes to the federal government to help offset its costs, and a guarantee fee, which goes to a guaranty agency for insuring the loan. Both are deducted from the amount given to you.

3. *Will you have to make any payments while still in school?* Usually you won't, and, depending on the type of loan, the government may even pay the interest for you while you're in school.

4. *What is the grace period—the period after my schooling ends, during which no payment is required?* Is it long enough, realistically, for you to find a job and get on your feet? (A six-month grace period is common.)

5. *When will my first payment be due, and approximately how much will it be?* You can get a good preview of the repayment process from the answer to these questions.

6. *Who exactly will hold my loan? To whom will I be sending payments?* Whom should I contact with questions or inform of changes in my situation? Your loan may be sold by the original lender to a secondary market institution.

7. *Will I have the right to pre-pay the loan, without penalty, at any time?* Some loan programs allow pre-payment with no penalty, but others do not.

8. *Will deferments and forbearances be possible if I am temporarily unable to make payments?* You need to find out how to apply for a deferment or forbearance if you need it.

9. *Will the loan be canceled ("forgiven") if I become totally and permanently disabled, or if I die?* This is always a good option to have on any loan you take out.

Federal Perkins Loans

A federal Perkins loan has the lowest interest (5%) of any loan available for both undergraduate and graduate students and is offered to students with exceptional financial need. You repay your school, who lends the money to you with government funds. Depending on when you apply, your level of need, and the funding level of the school, you can borrow up to $3,000 for each year of undergraduate study. The total amount you can borrow as an undergraduate is $15,000.

The school pays you directly by check or credits your tuition account. You have nine months after you graduate (provided you were continuously enrolled at least half-time) to begin repayment, with up to 10 years to pay off the entire loan.

PLUS Loans (Loans for Parents)

PLUS loans enable parents with good credit histories to borrow money to pay the education expenses of a child who is a dependent undergraduate student enrolled at least half time. Your parents must submit the completed forms to your school.

To be eligible, your parents will be required to pass a credit check. If they don't pass the credit check, they might still be able to receive a loan if they can show that extenuating circumstances exist, or if someone who is able to pass the credit check agrees to co-sign the loan. Your parents must also meet citizenship requirements.

The yearly limit on a PLUS Loan is equal to your cost of attendance minus any other financial aid you receive. For instance, if your cost of attendance is $6,000 and you receive $4,000 in other financial aid, your parents could borrow up to, but no more than, $2,000. The interest rate varies, but is not to exceed 9% over the life of the loan. Your parents must begin repayment while you're still in school. There is no grace period.

Federal Stafford Loans

Federal Stafford loans are low-interest loans that are given to students who attend school at least half time. The lender of the loans is usually a bank or credit union; however, sometimes a school may be the lender. Stafford loans are either subsidized or unsubsidized.

Subsidized loans are awarded based on financial need. You will not be charged any interest before you begin repayment or during authorized periods of deferment. The federal government "subsidizes" the interest during these periods.

Unsubsidized loans are not awarded because of financial need. You'll be charged interest from the time the loan is disbursed until it is paid in full. If you allow the interest to accumulate, it will be capitalized—that is, the interest will be added to the principal amount of your loan, and additional interest will be based upon the higher amount. This will increase the amount you have to repay.

If you're a dependent undergraduate student, you can borrow up to:

- $2,625 if you're a first-year student enrolled in a program that is at least a full academic year.
- $3,500 if you've completed your first year of study and the remainder of your program is at least a full academic year.
- $5,500 a year if you've completed two years of study and the remainder of your program is at least a full academic year.

If you're an independent undergraduate student or a dependent student whose parents are unable to get a PLUS Loan, you can borrow up to:

- ♦ $6,625 if you're a first-year student enrolled in a program that is at least a full academic year.
- ♦ $7,500 if you've completed your first year of study and the remainder of your program is at least a full academic year.

There are many borrowing limit categories to these loans, depending on whether you get an unsubsidized or subsidized loan, your year in school, how long your program of study is, and whether you're independent or dependent. You can have both kinds of Stafford loans at the same time, but the total amount of money loaned at any given time cannot exceed $23,000. The interest rate varies, but should not exceed 8.25%. An origination fee for a Stafford loan is approximately 3 or 4% of the loan, and the fee will be deducted from each loan disbursement you receive. There is a six-month grace period after graduation before you must start repaying the loan.

Federal Direct Student Loans

You should be aware of federal direct student loans, which are a part of a relatively new program. The loans use essentially the same terms as the federal Stafford student loans and the PLUS loans for parents. However, in this case the U.S. Department of Education is the lender, rather than a bank. One advantage to federal direct student loans is that they offer a variety of repayment terms, such as a fixed monthly payment for ten years or a variable monthly payment for up to 25 years that is based on a percentage of income. Be aware that not all colleges participate in this loan program.

Guidelines for Managing Your Loans

Before you commit yourself to any loans, be sure to keep in mind that these are loans, not grants or scholarships, so plan ahead and make sure that you don't borrow more than you'll be able to repay. Estimate realistically how much you'll earn when you leave school and remember that you'll have other monthly obligations such as housing, food, and transportation expenses.

Once You're In School

Once you have your loan (or loans) and you're attending classes, don't forget about the responsibility of your loan. Keep a file of information on your loan that includes copies of all your loan documents and related correspondence, along with a record of all your payments. Open and read all mail that you receive about your education loan.

Remember also that you are obligated by law to notify both your Financial Aid Administrator (FAA) and the holder or servicer of your loan if there is a change in your:

- name
- address
- enrollment status (dropping to less than half-time means that you'll have to begin payment six months later)
- anticipated graduation date

After You Leave School

After you leave school you must begin repaying your student loan either immediately, or after the grace period. For example, if you have a Stafford loan you will be provided with a six-month grace period before your first payment is due; other types of loans have grace periods as well. And, if you haven't been out in the world of work before, you'll begin your credit history with your loan repayment. If you make payments on time, you'll build up a good credit rating, and credit will be easier for you to obtain for other things. Get off to a good start, so you don't run the risk of going into default. If you default (or refuse to pay back your loan) any number of the following things could happen to you as a result:

- have trouble getting any kind of credit in the future
- no longer qualify for federal or state educational financial aid
- have holds placed on your college records
- have your wages garnished
- have future federal income tax refunds taken
- have your assets seized

To avoid the negative consequences of going into default on your loan, be sure to do the following:

- Open and read all mail you receive about your education loans immediately.
- Make scheduled payments on time. Since interest is calculated daily, delays can be costly.

- Contact your servicer immediately if you can't make payments on time. Your servicer may be able to get you into a graduated or income-sensitive/income-contingent repayment plan or work with you to arrange a deferment or forbearance. In spite of the horror stories you might hear, loan officials can be quite helpful if you don't try to evade your responsibility.

There are very few circumstances under which you won't have to repay your loan. If you become permanently and totally disabled, you probably will not have to (providing the disability did not exist prior to your obtaining the aid). Likewise if you die, if your school closes permanently in the middle of the term, or if you are erroneously certified for aid by the financial aid office. However, if you're simply disappointed in your program of study or don't get the job you wanted after graduation, you are not relieved of your obligation.

Remember, too, that there are restrictions on how you can use your loan money. It's to be used strictly for education-related expenses (for example, tuition, fees, books, room and board, transportation, and so on). A CD of your favorite rock band now and then won't hurt, or if you really need a toaster oven you can get by with that. But don't use your loan to buy expensive clothing, fund elaborate vacations, or buy a new car.

Loan Repayment

When it comes time to repay your loan, you will make payments to your original lender, to a secondary market institution to which your lender has sold your loan, or to a loan servicing specialist acting as its agent to collect payments.

At the beginning of the process, try to choose the lender who offers you the best benefits (for example, a lender who lets you pay electronically, offers lower interest rates to those who consistently pay on time, or who has a toll-free number to call 24 hours a day, 7 days a week). Ask the financial aid administrator at your college to direct you to such lenders.

Be sure to check out your repayment options before borrowing. Lenders are required to offer repayment plans that will make it easier to pay back your loans. Your repayment options may include:

- **Standard repayment:** full principal and interest payments due each month throughout your loan term. You'll pay the least amount of interest using the standard repayment plan, but your monthly payments may seem high when you're just out of school.

- **Graduated repayment:** interest-only or partial interest monthly payments due early in repayment. Payment amounts increase thereafter. Some lenders offer interest-only or partial interest repayment options which provide the lowest initial monthly payments available.

- **Income-based repayment:** monthly payments are based on a percentage of your monthly income.

- **Consolidation loan:** allows the borrower to consolidate several types of federal student loans with various repayment schedules into one loan. This loan is designed to help student or parent borrowers simplify their loan repayments. The interest rate on a consolidation loan may be lower than what you're currently paying on one or more of your loans. The phone number for loan consolidation at the William D. Ford Direct Loan Program is 800-557-7392. Financial administrators recommend that you do not consolidate a Perkins loan with any other loans since the interest on a Perkins loan is already the lowest available. Loan consolidation is not available from all lenders.

- **Prepayment:** paying more than is required on your loan each month or in a lump sum is allowed for all federally-sponsored loans at any time during the life of the loan without penalty. Prepayment will reduce the total cost of your loan.

It's quite possible—in fact likely—that while you're still in school your loan will be sold by the original lender to a secondary market institution. You'll be notified of the sale by letter, and you need not worry if this happens—your loan terms and conditions will remain exactly the same or they may even improve. Indeed, the sale may give you repayment options and benefits that you would not have had otherwise. Your payments and your requests for information should be directed to the new loan holder.

If you receive any interest-bearing student loans, you will have to attend exit counseling after graduation, where the loan lenders will tell you the total amount of debt and work out a payment schedule with you to determine the amount and dates of repayment. Many loans do not become due until six to nine months after you graduate, giving you a grace period. For example, you do not have to begin paying on the Perkins loan until nine months after you graduate. This grace period is to give you time to find a good job and start earning money. However, during this time, you may have to pay the interest on your loan.

If for some reason you remain unemployed when your payments become due, you may receive an unemployment deferment for a certain length of time. For many loans, you will have a maximum repayment period of 10 years (excluding periods of deferment and forbearance).

FINANCIAL AID QUESTIONS AND ANSWERS

Here are answers to the most frequently asked questions about student financial aid:

1. *I probably don't qualify for aid—should I apply for it anyway?* Yes. Many students and families mistakenly think they don't qualify for aid and fail to apply. Remember that there are some sources of aid that are not based on need. The FAFSA form is free—there's no good reason for not applying.

2. *Do I need to be admitted at a particular university before I can apply for financial aid?* No. You can apply for financial aid any time after January 1. However, to get the funds, you must be admitted and enrolled in a school.

3. *Do I have to reapply for financial aid every year?* Yes, and if your financial circumstances change, you may get either more or less aid. After your first year you will receive a "Renewal Application" which contains preprinted information from the previous year's FAFSA. Renewal of your aid also depends on your making satisfactory progress toward a degree and achieving a minimum GPA.

4. *Are my parents responsible for my educational loans?* No. You and you alone are responsible, unless your parents or another party endorse or co-sign your loan. Parents are, however, responsible for the federal PLUS loans. If your parents (or grandparents or uncle or distant cousins) want to help pay off your loan, you can have your billing statements sent to their address.

5. *If I take a leave of absence from school, do I have to start repaying my loans?* Not immediately, but you will after the grace period. Generally, though, if you use your grace period up during your leave, you'll have to begin repayment immediately after graduation, unless you apply for an extension of the grace period before it's used up.

6. *If I get assistance from another source, should I report it to the student financial aid office?* Yes, definitely—and, sadly, your aid amount will

probably be lowered accordingly. But you'll get into trouble later on if you don't report it.

7. *Where can I get information about federal student financial aid?* Call 1-800-4-FED-AID (1-800-433-3243) or 1-800-730-8913 (if hearing impaired) and ask for a free copy of *The Student Guide: Financial Aid from the U.S. Department of Education.* You can also request information from the Federal Student Aid Information Center, P.O. Box 84, Washington, DC 20044.

8. *Are federal work-study earnings taxable?* Yes, you must pay federal and state income tax (that is, if your state has an income tax!), although you may be exempt from FICA taxes if you are enrolled full time and work less than 20 hours a week.

9. *Where can I obtain a copy of the FAFSA?* Your guidance counselor should have the forms available. You can also get the FAFSA from the financial aid office at a local college, your local public library, or by calling 1-800-4-FED-AID.

10. *Are photocopies of the FAFSA acceptable?* No. Only the original FAFSA form produced by the U.S. Department of Education is acceptable. Photocopies, reproductions, and faxes are not acceptable.

11. *My parents are separated or divorced. Which parent is responsible for filling out the FAFSA?* If your parents are separated or divorced, the custodial parent is responsible for filling out the FAFSA. The custodial parent is the parent with whom you lived the most during the past 12 months. Note that this is not necessarily the same as the parent who has legal custody. The question of which parent must fill out the FAFSA becomes complicated in many situations, so you should take your particular circumstance to the student financial aid office for help.

Financial Aid Checklist

____ Explore your options as soon as possible after you've decided to begin a training program.

____ Find out what your school requires and what financial aid it offers.

____ Complete and mail the FAFSA as soon as possible after January 1.

____ Complete and mail other applications by the deadlines.

____ Gather loan application information and forms from your college financial aid office.

____ Forward the certified loan application to a participating lender: bank, savings and loan institution, or credit union, if necessary.

____ Carefully read all letters and notices from the school, the federal student aid processor, the need analysis service, and private scholarship organizations. Note whether financial aid will be sent before or after you are notified about admission, and how exactly you will receive the money.

____ Report any changes in your financial resources or expenses to your financial aid office so they can adjust your award accordingly.

____ Re-apply each year.

Financial Aid Acronyms Key

COA	Cost of Attendance
CWS	College Work-Study
EFC	Expected Family Contribution
EFT	Electronic Funds Transfer
ESAR	Electronic Student Aid Report
ETS	Educational Testing Service
FAA	Financial Aid Administrator
FAF	Financial Aid Form
FAFSA	Free Application for Federal Student Aid
FAO	Financial Aid Office
FDSLP	Federal Direct Student Loan Program
FFELP	Federal Family Education Loan Program
FSEOG	Federal Supplemental Educational Opportunity Grant
FWS	Federal Work-Study
GSL	Guaranteed Student Loan
PC	Parent Contribution
PLUS	Parent Loan for Undergraduate Students
SAP	Satisfactory Academic Progress
SC	Student Contribution
SLS	Supplemental Loan for Students

GLOSSARY OF FINANCIAL AID TERMS

Accrued interest: Interest that accumulates on the unpaid principal balance of your loan

Capitalization of interest: Addition of accrued interest to the principal balance of your loan which increases both your total debt and monthly payments

Default: Failure to repay your education loan

Deferment: A period when a borrower, who meets certain criteria, may suspend loan payments

Delinquency: Failure to make payments when due

Disbursement: Loan funds issued by the lender

Forbearance: Temporary adjustment to repayment schedule for cases of financial hardship

Grace period: Specified period of time after you graduate or leave school during which you need not make payments

Holder: The institution that currently owns your loan

In-school grace, and deferment interest subsidy: Interest the federal government pays for borrowers on some loans while the borrower is in school, during authorized deferments, and during grace periods

Interest-only payment: A payment that covers only interest owed on the loan and none of the principal balance

Interest: Cost you pay to borrow money

Lender (Originator): Puts up the money when you take out a loan. Most lenders are financial institutions, but some state agencies and schools make loans too.

Origination fee: Fee, deducted from the principal, that is paid to the federal government to offset its cost of the subsidy to borrowers under certain loan programs

Principal: Amount you borrow (which may increase as a result of capitalization of interest), and the amount on which you pay interest

Promissory note: Contract between you and the lender that includes all the terms and conditions under which you promise to repay your loan

Secondary markets: Institutions that buy student loans from originating lenders, thus providing lenders with funds to make new loans

Servicer: Organization that administers and collects your loan—either the holder of your loan or an agent acting on behalf of the holder

Tuition Reimbursement: Tuition reimbursement programs pay all or most of required expenses for employees to obtain a higher certification or degree.

FINANCIAL AID RESOURCES

Here are several additional resources that you can use to obtain more information about financial aid. In addition, check out Appendix B for more reading materials you may want to review.

Telephone Numbers

These phone numbers may be of help to you when completing your financial aid application forms:

Federal Student Aid Information Center (U.S. Department of Education)

Hotline 800-4-FED-AID (800-433-3243)

TDD (Number for hearing-impaired) 800-730-8913

For suspicion of fraud or abuse of federal aid....800-MIS-USED (800-647-8733)

Selective Service...847-688-6888

Immigration and Naturalization (INS) 415-705-4205

Internal Revenue Service (IRS) 800-829-1040

Social Security Administration..800-772-1213

National Merit Scholarship Corporation 708-866-5100

Sallie Mae's College AnswerSM Service...............................800-222-7183

Career College Association 202-336-6828

ACT: American College Testing program................................916-361-0656

College Scholarship Service (CSS) ....609-771-7725; TDD 609-883-7051

Need Access/Need Analysis Service.......................................800-282-1550

FAFSA on the Web Processing/Software Problems..............................800-801-0576

Web Sites

Check out these Web sites for information about financial aid:

http://www.ed.gov/prog_info/SFAStudentGuide.
The *Student Guide* is a free informative brochure about financial aid and is available on-line at the Department of Education's Web address listed here.

http://www.ed.gov\prog_info\SFA\FAFSA
This site offers students help in completing the FAFSA.

http://www.ed.gov/offices/OPE/t4_codes.html.
This site offers a list of Title IV school codes that you may need to complete the FAFSA.

http://www.ed.gov/offices/OPE/express.html

This site enables you to fill out and submit the FAFSA on-line. You'll need to print out, sign, and send in the release and signature pages.

http://www.finaid.org/finaid

This is one of the most comprehensive Web sites for financial aid information. They have many pages addressing special situations, such as international students, bankruptcy, defaulting on student loans, divorced parents, financially unsupportive parents, and myths about financial aid.

http://www.finaid.org/finaid/phone.html

This site lists telephone numbers specific to loan programs, loan consolidations, tuition payment plans, and state prepaid tuition plans.

http://www.finaid.org/finaid/documents.html

Free on-line documents can be found at this site.

http://www.finaid.org/finaid/vendors/software.html

Software for EFC calculators and financial aid planning and advice are at this site.

http://www.career.org

This is the Web site of the Career College Association (CCA). The CCA offers a limited number of scholarships for attendance at private proprietary schools. Contact CCA for further information at 750 First Street, NE, Suite 900, Washington, DC 20002-4242, or visit their Web site.

http://www.salliemae.com

The Web site for Sallie Mae contains information about loan programs.

http://www.fastweb.com

This site is called FastWEB. If you answer a few simple questions for them (such as name and address, geographical location, associations and organizations that you are affiliated with, age, and so on), they will give you a free list of possible scholarships you might qualify for. Their database is updated regularly, and your list gets updated when new scholarships are added that fit your profile. FastWEB boasts that more than 20,000 students access their site every day.

Scholarship Search Services

If you find financial aid information overwhelming, or if you simply don't have the time to do the footwork yourself, you may want to hire a scholarship search service. Be aware that a reasonable price is $30-$50. If the service wants to charge more, investigate it carefully. Scholarship search services usually only provide you with a list of six or so sources of scholarships that you then need to check out and apply for.

Software Programs

Cash for Class
800-205-9581
Fax: 714-673-9039

Redheads Software, Inc.
3334 East Coast Highway #216
Corona del Mar, CA 92625
E-mail: cashclass@aol.com

C-LECT Financial Aid Module
Chronicle Guidance Publications
P.O. Box 1190
Moravia, NY 13118-1190
315-497-0330 / 800-622-7284
Fax: 315-497-3359

Peterson's Award Search
Peterson's
P.O. Box 2123
Princeton, NJ 08543-2123
609-243-9111 / 800-338-3282
E-mail: custsvc@petersons.com

Pinnacle Peak Solutions (Scholarships 101)
Pinnacle Peak Solutions
7735 East Windrose Drive
Scottsdale, AZ 85260
602-951-9377 / 800-762-7101
Fax: 602-948-7603

TP Software—Student Financial Aid Search Software
TP Software
P.O. Box 532
Bonita, CA 91908-0532
619-496-8673 / 800-791-7791
E-mail: mail@tpsoftware.com

Books and Pamphlets

Take a look at any of the following books and pamphlets to get more information about the financial aid process:

The Student Guide
Published by the U.S. Department of Education, this is the handbook about federal aid programs. To get a printed copy, call 1-800-4-FED-AID.

Looking for Student Aid
Published by the U.S. Department of Education, this is an overview of sources of information about financial aid. To get a printed copy, call 1-800-4-FED-AID.

How Can I Receive Financial Aid for College?
Published from the Parent Brochures ACCESS ERIC Web site. Order a printed copy by calling 800-LET-ERIC or write to ACCESS ERIC, Research Blvd-MS 5F, Rockville, MD 20850-3172.

The Best Resources for College Financial Aid 1996/97 by Michael Osborn. Published by Resource Pathways Inc., 1996. This book lists resources available to students, parents, and counselors—books, Web sites, CD-ROMs, videos, software—and then recommends the most useful for each stage in the financial aid search. It includes a concise description and evaluation of each resource.

10-Minute Guide to Paying for College by William D. Van Dusen and Bart Astor. Published by Arco Publishing, 1996. A quick, simple, step-by-step guide for getting through the financial aid process that answers the most pressing financial aid questions. Both parents and students will appreciate this easy-to-use book.

College Financial Aid for Dummies by Herm Davis and Joyce Kennedy. Published by IDG Books Worldwide, 1997. This fun and friendly reference guides readers through the financial aid maze by covering the major types of loans, grants, and scholarships available with strategies for how to find and secure them.

Other Financial Aid Books

- *Annual Register of Grant Support.* Chicago: Marquis, Annual.
- *A's and B's of Academic Scholarships.* Alexandria, VA: Octameron, Annual.
- *Chronicle Student Aid Annual.* Moravia, NY: Chronicle Guidance, Annual.
- *College Blue Book: Scholarships, Fellowships, Grants and Loans.* New York: Macmillan, Annual.
- *College Scholarships and Financial Aid.* New York: Arco, Annual.
- *Directory of Financial Aid for Minorities.* San Carlos, CA: Reference Service Press, Biennial.
- *Directory of Financial Aid for Women.* San Carlos, CA: Reference Service Press, Biennial
- *Don't Miss Out: the Ambitious Student's Guide to Financial Aid.* Alexandria, VA: Octameron, Annual.
- *Financial Aid for Higher Education.* Dubuque: Wm. C. Brown, Biennial.
- *Financial Aid for the Disabled and their Families.* San Carlos, CA: Reference Service Press, Biennial.

Free Application for Federal Student Aid
1997–98 School Year

WARNING: If you purposely give false or misleading information on this form, you may be fined $10,000, sent to prison, or both.

"You" and "your" on this form always mean the student who wants aid.

Form Approved
OMB No. 1840-0110
App. Exp. 6/30/98

U.S. Department of Education
Student Financial
Assistance Programs

Use dark ink. Make capital letters and numbers clear and legible. `E X M 2 4`

Fill in ovals completely. Only one oval per question. Correct ●

Incorrect marks will be ignored. Incorrect ✗ ✓

Section A: You (the student)

1–3. Your name

1. Last name
2. First name
3. M.I.

Your title (optional) Mr. ○ 1 Miss, Mrs., or Ms. ○ 2

4–7. Your permanent mailing address
(All mail will be sent to this address. See Instructions, page 2 for state/country abbreviations.)

4. Number and street (Include apt. no.)

5. City
6. State
7. ZIP code

8. Your social security number (SSN) *(Don't leave blank. See Instructions, page 2.)*

9. Your date of birth
Month Day Year
1 9

10. Your permanent home telephone number
Area code

11. Your state of legal residence
State

12. Date you became a legal resident of the state in question 11 *(See Instructions, page 2.)*
Month Day Year
1 9

13–14. Your driver's license number *(Include the state abbreviation. If you don't have a license, write in "None.")*
State License number

15–16. Are you a U.S. citizen?
(See Instructions, pages 2–3.)
Yes, I am a U.S. citizen. ○ 1
No, but I am an eligible noncitizen. ○ 2
A
No, neither of the above. ○ 3

17. As of today, are you married? *(Fill in only one oval.)*
I am not married. (I am single, widowed, or divorced.) ○ 1
I am married. ○ 2
I am separated from my spouse. ○ 3

18. Date you were married, separated, divorced, or widowed. If divorced, use date of divorce or separation, whichever is earlier.
(If never married, leave blank.) Month Year
1 9

19. Will you have your first bachelor's degree before July 1, 1997?
Yes ○ 1
No ○ 2

Section B: Education Background

20–21. Date that you (the student) received, or will receive, your high school diploma, either—
*(Enter **one** date. Leave blank if the question does not apply to you.)*

• by graduating from high school **20.**
Month Year
1 9

OR

• by earning a GED **21.**
Month Year
1 9

22–23. Highest educational level or grade level your father and your mother completed. *(Fill in one oval for each parent. See Instructions, page 3.)*

	22. Father	23. Mother
elementary school (K–8)	○ 1	○ 1
high school (9–12)	○ 2	○ 2
college or beyond	○ 3	○ 3
unknown	○ 4	○ 4

If you (and your family) have **unusual circumstances**, complete this form and then check with your financial aid administrator. Examples:

• tuition expenses at an elementary or secondary school,
• unusual medical or dental expenses not covered by insurance,

• a family member who recently became unemployed, or
• other unusual circumstances such as changes in income or assets that might affect your eligibility for student financial aid.

Section C: Your Plans *Answer these questions about your college plans.* *Page 2*

24–28. Your expected enrollment status for the 1997–98 school year
(See Instructions, page 3.)

School term	Full time	3/4 time	1/2 time	Less than 1/2 time	Not enrolled
24. Summer term '97	○ 1	○ 2	○ 3	○ 4	○ 5
25. Fall semester/qtr. '97	○ 1	○ 2	○ 3	○ 4	○ 5
26. Winter quarter '97-98	○ 1	○ 2	○ 3	○ 4	○ 5
27. Spring semester/qtr. '98	○ 1	○ 2	○ 3	○ 4	○ 5
28. Summer term '98	○ 1	○ 2	○ 3	○ 4	○ 5

29. Your course of study *(See Instructions for code, page 3.)* Code [ ]

30. College degree/certificate you expect to receive *(See Instructions for code, page 3.)* [ ]

31. Date you expect to receive your degree/certificate — Month [ ] Day [ ] Year [ ]

32. Your grade level during the 1997–98 school year *(Fill in only one.)*

- 1st yr/never attended college ○ 1
- 1st yr./attended college before ○ 2
- 2nd year/sophomore ○ 3
- 3rd year/junior ○ 4
- 4th year/senior ○ 5
- 5th year/other undergraduate ○ 6
- 1st year graduate/professional ○ 7
- 2nd year graduate/professional ○ 8
- 3rd year graduate/professional ○ 9
- Beyond 3rd year graduate/professional ○ 10

33–35. In addition to grants, what other types of financial aid are you (and your parents) interested in? *(See Instructions, page 3.)*

33. Student employment — Yes ○ 1 No ○ 2

34. Student loans — Yes ○ 1 No ○ 2

35. Parent loans for students — Yes ○ 1 No ○ 2

36. If you are (or were) in college, do you plan to attend **that same college** in 1997–98? *(If this doesn't apply to you, leave blank.)* — Yes ○ 1 No ○ 2

37. For how many dependents will you (the student) pay child care or elder care expenses in 1997–98? [ ]

38–39. Veterans education benefits you expect to receive from July 1, 1997 through June 30, 1998

38. Amount per month $[ ].00

39. Number of months [ ]

Section D: Student Status

40. Were you born **before** January 1, 1974? .... Yes ○ 1 No ○ 2

41. Are you a veteran of the U.S. Armed Forces? .... Yes ○ 1 No ○ 2

42. Will you be enrolled in a graduate or professional program (beyond a bachelor's degree) in 1997-98? .... Yes ○ 1 No ○ 2

43. Are you married? .... Yes ○ 1 No ○ 2

44. Are you an orphan or a ward of the court, or **were** you a ward of the court until age 18? .... Yes ○ 1 No ○ 2

45. Do you have legal dependents (**other than a spouse**) that fit the definition in Instructions, page 4? .... Yes ○ 1 No ○ 2

If you answered "Yes" to **any** question in Section D, go to Section E and fill out **both the GRAY and the WHITE** areas on the rest of this form.

If you answered "No" to **every** question in Section D, go to Section E and fill out **both the GREEN and the WHITE** areas on the rest of this form.

Section E: Household Information

Remember:
At least one "Yes" answer in Section D means fill out the **GRAY** and WHITE areas.

All "No" answers in Section D means fill out the **GREEN** and WHITE areas.

STUDENT (& SPOUSE)

46. Number in your household in 1997–98 *(Include yourself and your spouse. Do not include your children and other people unless they meet the definition in Instructions, page 4.)* [ ]

47. Number of college students in household in 1997–98 *(Of the number in 46, how many will be in college at least half-time in at least one term in an eligible program? Include yourself. See Instructions, page 4.)* [ ]

PARENT(S)

48. Your parent(s)' **current** marital status:

- single ○ 1
- married ○ 2
- separated ○ 3
- divorced ○ 4
- widowed ○ 5

49. Your parent(s)' state of legal residence — State [ ]

50. Date your parent(s) became legal resident(s) of the state in question 49 *(See Instructions, page 5.)* — Month [ ] Day [ ] Year [1 9]

51. Number in your parent(s)' household in 1997–98 *(Include yourself and your parents. Do not include your parents' other children and other people unless they meet the definition in Instructions, page 5.)* [ ]

52. Number of college students in household in 1997–98 *(Of the number in 51, how many will be in college at least half-time in at least one term in an eligible program? Include yourself. See Instructions, page 5.)* [ ]

Section F: 1996 Income, Earnings, and Benefits *You must see Instructions, pages 5 and 6, for information about tax forms and tax filing status, especially if you are estimating taxes or filing electronically or by telephone. These instructions will tell you what income and benefits should be reported in this section.* *Page 3*

	STUDENT (& SPOUSE) *Everyone must fill out this column.*	PARENT(S)
The following 1996 U.S. income tax figures are from:	53. *(Fill in one oval.)*	65. *(Fill in one oval.)*
A—a completed 1996 IRS Form 1040A, 1040EZ, or 1040TEL	○ 1	A ○ 1
B—a completed 1996 IRS Form 1040	○ 2	B ○ 2
C—an estimated 1996 IRS Form 1040A, 1040EZ, or 1040TEL	○ 3	C ○ 3
D—an estimated 1996 IRS Form 1040	○ 4	D ○ 4
E—will not file a 1996 U.S. income tax return	*(Skip to question 57.)* ○ 5	E *(Skip to 69.)* ○ 5

TAX FILERS ONLY

	STUDENT (& SPOUSE)	PARENT(S)
1996 Total number of exemptions (Form 1040–line 6d, or 1040A–line 6d; 1040EZ filers— *see Instructions, page 6.*)	54.	66.
1996 Adjusted Gross Income (AGI: Form 1040–line 31, 1040A–line 16, or 1040EZ–line 4 —*see Instructions, page 6.*)	55. $ .00	67. $ .00
1996 U.S. income tax **paid** (Form 1040–line 44, 1040A–line 25, or 1040EZ–line 10)	56. $ .00	68. $ .00
1996 Income earned from work	(Student) 57. $ .00	(Father) 69. $ .00
1996 Income earned from work	(Spouse) 58. $ .00	(Mother) 70. $ .00

1996 Untaxed income and benefits (yearly totals only):

	STUDENT (& SPOUSE)	PARENT(S)
Earned Income Credit (Form 1040–line 54, Form 1040A–line 29c, or Form 1040EZ–line 8)	59. $ .00	71. $ .00
Untaxed Social Security Benefits	60. $ .00	72. $ .00
Aid to Families with Dependent Children (AFDC/ADC)	61. $ .00	73. $ .00
Child support received for all children	62. $ .00	74. $ .00
Other untaxed income and benefits from Worksheet #2, page 11	63. $ .00	75. $ .00
1996 Amount from Line 5, Worksheet #3, page 12 *(See Instructions.)*	64. $ .00	76. $ .00

Section G: Asset Information   **ATTENTION!**

Fill out Worksheet A or Worksheet B in Instructions, page 7. *If you meet the tax filing and income conditions on Worksheets A and B, you do not have to complete Section G to apply for Federal student aid. Some states and colleges, however, require Section G information for their own aid programs. Check with your financial aid administrator and/or State Agency.*

Age of your older parent **84.**

	STUDENT (& SPOUSE)	PARENT(S)
Cash, savings, and checking accounts	77. $ .00	85. $ .00
Other real estate and investments value *(Don't include the home.)*	78. $ .00	86. $ .00
Other real estate and investments debt *(Don't include the home.)*	79. $ .00	87. $ .00
Business value	80. $ .00	88. $ .00
Business debt	81. $ .00	89. $ .00
Investment farm value *(See Instructions, page 8.)* *(Don't include a family farm.)*	82. $ .00	90. $ .00
Investment farm debt *(See Instructions, page 8.)* *(Don't include a family farm.)*	83. $ .00	91. $ .00

SAMPLE

Section H: Releases and Signatures

92–103. What college(s) do you plan to attend in 1997–98?

(Note: The colleges you list below will have access to your application information. See Instructions, page 8.)

Housing codes	1—on-campus	3—with parent(s)
	2—off-campus	4—with relative(s) other than parent(s)

	Title IV School Code	College Name	College Street Address and City	State	Housing Code
XX.	0 5 4 3 2 1	EXAMPLE UNIVERSITY	14930 NORTH SOMEWHERE BLVD. ANYWHERE CITY	S T	XX. 2
92.					93.
94.					95.
96.					97.
98.					99.
100.					101.
102.					103.

104. The U.S. Department of Education will send information from this form to your state financial aid agency and the state agencies of the colleges listed above so they can consider you for state aid. Answer **"No"** if you **don't** want information released to the state. *(See Instructions, page 9 and "Deadlines for State Student Aid," page 10.)* ....**104.** No ◯ 2

105. Males not yet registered for Selective Service (SS): Do you want SS to register you? *(See Instructions, page 9.)* ....**105.** Yes ◯ 1

106–107. Read, Sign, and Date Below

All of the information provided by me or any other person on this form is true and complete to the best of my knowledge. I understand that this application is being filed jointly by all signatories. If asked by an authorized official, I agree to give proof of the information that I have given on this form. I realize that this proof may include a copy of my U.S. or state income tax return. I also realize that if I do not give proof when asked, the student may be denied aid.

Statement of Educational Purpose. I certify that I will use any Federal Title IV, HEA funds I receive during the award year covered by this application solely for expenses related to my attendance at the institution of higher education that determined or certified my eligibility for those funds.

Certification Statement on Overpayments and Defaults. I understand that I may not receive any Federal Title IV, HEA funds if I owe an overpayment on any Title IV educational grant or loan or am in default on a Title IV educational loan unless I have made satisfactory arrangements to repay or otherwise resolve the overpayment or default. I also understand that I must notify my school if I do owe an overpayment or am in default.

Everyone whose information is given on this form should sign below. The student (and at least one parent, if parental information is given) must sign below or this form will be returned unprocessed.

106. Signatures *(Sign in the boxes below.)*

¹ Student

² Student's Spouse

³ Father/Stepfather

⁴ Mother/Stepmother

107. Date completed

Month	Day	Year
		1997 ◯
		1998 ◯

Section I: Preparer's Use Only

For preparers other than student, spouse, and parent(s). Student, spouse, and parent(s), sign in question 106.

Preparer's name (last, first, MI)

Firm name

Firm or preparer's address (street, city, state, ZIP)

108. Employer identification number (EIN)

OR

109. Preparer's social security number

Certification: All of the information on this form is true and complete to the best of my knowledge.

110. Preparer's signature Date

School Use Only

D/O ◯ Title IV Code

FAA Signature

MDE Use Only
Do not write in this box

Special handle

MAKE SURE THAT YOU HAVE COMPLETED, DATED, AND SIGNED THIS APPLICATION.

Mail the original application (NOT A PHOTOCOPY) to: Federal Student Aid Programs, P.O. Box 4008, Mt. Vernon, IL 62864-8608

THE INSIDE TRACK

Who:	Leonard Fechter
What:	Sales Associate, Sears Roebuck and Co.
Where:	Albuquerque, New Mexico
Education:	High school student, taking college classes at local two-year college

Insider's Advice

I started working for Sears when I turned 16, through a special program for high school students sponsored by the New Mexico Retailers Association. I've worked there for two years, and have never been late or absent. I was in receiving for a year, unloading trucks and doing package pickup, after school and weekends. I got real close to a lot of managers this way. I then transferred to hardware as a sales associate. Several managers were pushing me to get out on the sales floor. I wasn't sure I wanted to, but the manager hired me on the spot. I got a drop in pay but I'm also on commission. I've tripled my paycheck from what it was in receiving.

I work evenings and weekends; I have Wednesdays and Thursdays off. All sales associates greet customers, welcome them to the store, and find out what they need. I demonstrate options of the products—I specialize in power tools. I describe warrantees for product replacement or repair.

In this job you need to be able to talk to people. You have to be honest about the product you're selling, and you have to be persuasive. You give the customer the service that he really wants. You need a lot of energy to be able to talk all day long and run around.

Last summer I also worked as a sales clerk and film processor at Walgreens. At Sears we're expected to have a lot of product knowledge. I developed product knowledge by reading the booklets that describe the features and benefits of the products. We are tested on the features and benefits of the new products, as well as on our knowledge about the Sears Card.

I enjoy getting to meet a lot of people in a business atmosphere, relating to customers in a professional way. The pay is really good for someone my age.

Insider's Take on the Future

I look forward to being promoted at Sears. You need a college degree to be in management, and the company will pay 75% of your tuition if you're working part-time; and you can get a scholarship.

I'm going to transfer the credits I've earned at Albuquerque Technical Vocational Institute. I'm planning to attend New Mexico State University after graduation. I have a 3.5 GPA, and I think I have a good chance at getting scholarships at TVI this year. I want to major in business administration at NMSU. I want to be a CEO of a company, maybe own my own company someday, but I'm not sure about that yet.

CHAPTER | 5

This chapter explains how to land your first retailing job, whether you've completed a training program or are entering the workforce straight from high school or another career path. You'll learn how to conduct an effective job search using want ads, the Internet, hotlines, job and career fairs, and industry publications. You'll get tips on preparing your resume and cover letter and on interviewing. You'll also get information about networking, and inside advice from retailing professionals.

HOW TO LAND YOUR FIRST JOB

Whether you intend to get your first retail position without getting formal training, or have just completed your program, it's time to start looking for the job and organization that best fits your skills, interests, and personality.

And don't let this stage of the game make you nervous. Yes, job hunting isn't the most enjoyable pastime for most people, but you can do it! You've come this far, and there are tons of jobs in retail. It's a booming industry, employing one out of five workers in the United States.

Ready? Set? Let's go!

ORGANIZING YOURSELF

Before doing anything, gather together all the information that can help you present yourself effectively to an employer. Use a 12-pocket folder or set of file folders (or 9 x 12 manila envelopes), all available at office supply stores and many discount stores, to help you systematically store and organize your educational and work credentials.

Label and include the following kinds of documents in your "career portfolio" folder(s):

* certificates/diplomas earned
* financial aid forms
* list of references (with names, addresses, and phone numbers)
* letters of recommendation
* resume
* sample completed job and/or college application
* school special awards
* standardized admissions/placement test scores
* transcripts
* workplace basics (see box on next page)

Listed here are types of skills and abilities retailers want their employees to have. Identify the types of skills you already have, and then identify the areas you need to work on.

Once you've got a handle on these materials, it will be easier to ready yourself for replying to want ads, completing job applications, and participating in job interviews.

CONDUCTING YOUR JOB SEARCH

Finding a sales associate or similar job in retailing can be as easy as cruising the mall. Finding the *right* job, however, usually requires research. By using the right techniques, you can identify and evaluate the opportunities that exist in the area where you want to work, and confidently land the job you want. Keep reading for tips on maximizing your job hunting success.

Walk Right In

There are retail establishments everywhere you look. If you have shopped in a particular store and think you might like to work there, put on job-seeking attire,

Workplace Basics*

TYPES OF SKILLS	SKILLS I HAVE	SKILLS I NEED
Reading skills use of print resource material for obtaining and applying information		
Writing Skills written communication of processes, information, or ideas		
Mathematics Skills computation, calculation, and interpretation of numerical data		
Computer Science Skills mastery and application of computer information or theory		
Oral Communication Skills speaking and listening		
Interpersonal or Relating Skills working and getting along with others, working in teams, leadership, and negotiation skills		
Creative Thinking and Problem Solving Skills comprehending, applying, analyzing, and developing complex ideas and situations		
Other Retail Skills specific skills used in a retailing environment: display, inventory, handling money, cash registers, loss prevention, etc.		

*Adapted from a checklist developed by Carnevale, Anthony, et al. *Workplace Basics: The Skills Employers Want.* Alexandria, VA. The American Society for Training and Development. 1991.

prepare your resume, put a smile on your face and march right up to the manager or the personnel department and ask about job opportunities.

If you don't know how to find the right person to speak with, here's a tip. Neal Lenarsky, a retailing industry executive recruiter in Woodland Hills, California, advises job seekers who are interested in working at a particular store to walk in and talk to a sales associate on the floor. Say, "I'd like to talk to the manager about any openings that might be coming up."

Help-Wanted Ads

The classified ads in your local newspaper are an easy and inexpensive way to job hunt. The paper is delivered to your doorstep, and it's bound to contain ads for lots of retailing positions. Look in the index to the classified ads, if available, to see what kinds of help wanted ads are posted under which headings. Depending on how the editor organizes job openings, look under headings such as "Sales," "Customer Service," "Cashier," "Retail," "Hospitality," or any other catagories that seem applicable. Check under "Temporary" or "Part Time" job postings as well; you never know when an employer will like you enough from your work during evenings, weekends, summers, or holidays to offer you a full-time job.

Regardless of what the index shows you, it's a good idea to browse your newspaper's want ad section to see how retailing positions may be advertised. In larger communities you may find retail openings advertised in the paper's Business, Living, or Fashion sections, as well as the classifieds. Remember, employers try to place their ads where they expect the kind of person they want to recruit will read them. So, a store might publish a "help wanted" advertisement as part of the general announcement about a grand opening sale or other event.

When you find an opening that interests you, follow the instructions given. You may be invited to call; or you may be told to mail or fax your resume to the employer. Some employers encourage you to drop by the store to fill out an application; others explicitly instruct job seekers to correspond with them first.

If there is a phone number to call, it's a good idea to call first to learn the name of the person you can send your resume to (if that information isn't included in the ad). See the sections later in this chapter about resumes and cover letters for tips on how to prepare yourself for using these tools.

Here are three sample want ads. Look how each ad instructs you to respond in a different way.

FRIEDMAN'S JEWELERS The Value Leader. The 3rd largest and fastest growing retail jewelry chain is now hiring in the Wal-Mart plaza on Richmond Road. Now hiring FT & PT MANAGER TRAINEES. Previous jewelry experience desired...but will train. If you wish to join the winning team please call Bill Smith at 555-269-6387, Mon-Sat, 10a-7p.

Rite Aid Corp., one of the country's largest retail drugstore chains with over 10 billion dollars in annual sales, is seeking people with a minimum of two years retail management experience. We have over 35,000 drugstores, and we are still opening new stores. With a strict promotion-from-within policy, the opportunity for advancement is excellent. Rite Aid offers an attractive salary, fully comprehensive benefits package and a promising career to the right person. Prefer prior experiences in toy, HBA, fast food or supermarket. If you're a hard working, honest individual, please fax or mail your resume. 555-726-7277, or 23 Calvert Rd, Frederick, ME 13345.

WE ARE looking for a person who: 1) Knows what it means to give outstanding customer service, 2) Has an eye for fashion. WE OFFER: 1)The opportunity to manage the Men's Dept., 2) A chance to enjoy a competitive wage & benefit package, 3) All the training you need to succeed with us. Dawahares, a leading retailer in Lexington, has a FT position in Sales/Mgmt. If you want to learn about retail for a future career and would like to grow with us, we should talk. Apply in person. We are located at the corner of Smith and Hoyt Streets.

Once you've contacted the company as instructed, schedule a date a couple of weeks in the future to follow up on the status of your application. If you don't get some kind of response back (a phone call, a postcard, or letter) write a polite note or call the company asking whether the job is still open.

Career Services

Most schools and colleges have a job placement or career-planning center. If you are a prospective or current student, or a recent graduate, take advantage of these resources.They are there to help students and graduates find a job and make the school look good. Their staffs usually have lots of information about current openings in the community. Many employers recruit employees from technical or trade schools and colleges. The centers usually have a job board or a job database that has information about jobs on and off-campus. They may hold job fairs that attract employers looking to hire energetic, skilled people (like you!) for entry-level positions and management training programs, and many retailers conduct on-campus interviews with students.

> ### Why College Career Centers are Great
>
> It's a good idea to get to know the career center at your school. Here are three good reasons why:
>
> 1. A career counselor or placement specialist can show you how to connect with internship sponsors and employers (some will be on the Internet, while others may come directly to your campus) all over the world.
>
> 2. You can network with graduates who can help you realize your career dreams and aspirations.
>
> 3. Most career centers will help you with your resume and cover letters, as well as conduct practice interviews with you and record them on videotape or audiotape.

State Employment Services and Temporary Agencies

Local and state employment services are another source of information about job openings in retailing, especially for part-time and temporary jobs, which could very well lead to full-time work. More than 2,700 of these centers are located throughout the country, and employers frequently keep their current openings posted there. Most have telephone job hotlines as well. Call your local state or employment service for the phone number of the hotline that offers lists of jobs in your area, or check the *National Job Hotline Directory: The Job Finder's Hot List* in the reference department of your public library.

Temporary work is a good way to find the right fit between you and a retail company. Temp agencies are worth checking out to see what kinds of retail employers they work with to place people for short-term assignments.

On-Line Resources

The Internet is a relatively new way to look for jobs, but it is one of the fastest-growing. There are over 8,000 sites available with jobs, employment opportunities, and career positions for anyone who has a computer and access to the Internet.

The Internet is a great resource to read the classified help wanted ads for newspapers from larger cities across the country, many of which are on-line and fully searchable, using key words such as "sales," "retail," and so on. In addition, you can use the search feature of your Internet browser (such as Netscape Communicator, Microsoft's Internet Explorer, etc.) to locate the World Wide Web site of a variety of retail organizations. When you find the Web site for, say,

JC Penney Co. (http://www.jcpenney.com), you may discover information about employment opportunities. Many corporations use their Web sites to recruit potential employees. There are several Web sites devoted to helping people find jobs. Some of the best are listed in the table below.

Job-related Internet Sites	
http://www.careermosaic.com	Jobs, employer profiles, online job fairs, job seeking tips
http://jobbankusa.com	Lots of jobs and related job-seeking info
http://www.careerpath.com	Research employers, search newspaper help-wanted ads, post your resume, more
http://www.monster.com:80/	Over 50,000 jobs and other help
http://www.jobweb.org/search/jobs/	Job leads and employer profiles
http://www.tripod.com/jobs_career/intern_visa/	A searchable internship database
http://interoz.com/usr/gcbristow/	Links to many job-finding sites, several quite specialized

Here is an example of a help wanted ad from careermosaic.com:

Employer:	CellularOne
Title:	Retail Sales Associate
Location:	San Francisco Bay Area, CA 94080, USA

Description: The Retail Sales Associate will provide equipment information and sell appropriate cellular telephone/accessories. This position will also interact with current subscribers by providing information on cellular telephone usage, billing, roaming, etc.

Associate sales duties include: Customer On The Move, assists, rate plan migrations, Enable-Link, out of market activations, referrals, churn-buster retention and referrals.

The Retail Sales Associate will also program cellular telephones, process ESN changes, provide loaner phones, and trouble shoot equipment problems.

Other duties will include compilation of personal equipment sales reports and monthly activity reports, maintenance of retail showroom, inventory, and cash drawer.

Requirements/Qualifications: The successful candidate will have strong personable communication skills with retail operations and sales experience. College degree preferred.

Using the Internet for job hunting is very appealing. You don't have to call anyone on the phone; you can stay inside where it's warm (or cool) and dry in your jammies and slippers; you can surf the Net at 2 a.m. Still, there's so much information out there, it's easy to get lost. Here are some tips:

+ Know what you're looking for; the more specific, the better. Some employers seem to be posting every position they have available. If you want to research or apply to a particular company—say, Nordstom, Home Depot or Radio Shack, go to their Web site and check out their job listings there. Take advantage of the knowledge you've accumulated about retailing and go seek out the places you'd like to work. Also, by knowing what job you want, you can save a lot of time at the Web job sites by entering the most specific search criteria you can. Even knowing what part of the country or what city you want to work in can save you a lot of time.

+ Have an ASCII (a plain-text document without any fancy formatting, readable by all computers) version of your resume available and ready to post. It's easier to prepare a careful, polished resume off-line, and then cut and paste your resume into the Web site while you're online.

+ Send a cover letter where possible. It's very tempting to simply hit a couple of buttons on your keyboard or click the mouse and send your resume off to a potential employer (or to thousands of employers). But a cover letter can tell a potential employer more about you than your resume alone, especially in a company where a personnel department receives hundreds or maybe thousands of responses to a single job posting. By taking the time to write a well-crafted cover letter, you'll illustrate that you have some knowledge about the company and can give some persuasive reasons why you should be considered for the job. This will give your resume a much better chance of actually being looked at!

Job Fairs

Many colleges and universities sponsor at least one job fair per year. In addition, trade groups, employers, or cities may hold job fairs in public places (malls, auditoriums, etc.) to allow local employers and potential employees to meet. These events are useful for students beginning to network and research potential employers, as well as for job seekers ready to start work immediately.

When you attend job fairs, wear business clothes, just as you will when you go to a scheduled job interview, and bring at least ten copies of your resume to distribute.

NETWORKING YOUR WAY INTO A JOB

Networking can be a great way to find job opportunities in retailing. It can open all kinds of new doors, just by having someone make an introduction or put in a good word. Keep reading on how to use this approach effectively.

What is Networking?

Networking means what it sounds like: spreading a "net" over a broad "sea" of potential "fish" to "catch" what you need. In this case, you're casting your net to find information that will lead you to a retailing position that meets your skills, interests, and goals.

Keep in mind that networking isn't about getting a job. To do that, you'll still need to fill out applications, submit a resume and cover letter, participate in interviews, and so on. Rather, networking is about finding people who may know about a company that has job openings, and about finding people who can put you in touch with the actual people doing the hiring. Many times employers will make job offers based on an endorsement by a current employee or someone else the employer trusts, because the employer respects the opinion of the person who introduced or recommended you to the employer.

Is networking a waste of time when you can walk into a store and speak directly to an owner or manager who has the power to hire you? Perhaps, *if* you already know exactly where you want to work and can contact the hiring manager directly. But, if you aren't sure where the right opening for you may be, or if you don't know how to contact the person hiring at your ideal company, then networking is an effective strategy.

Retail recruiter Tom Russell says, "Most jobs are found through some form of networking. Someone at the company has received some form of input about you from a reliable or credible source. Let's call it a referral."

Remember: for the rest of your life you have two choices: networking or not working.

Getting Useful Contacts

Start networking by talking with friends, family, classmates, acquaintances, teachers, former employers, neighbors, and anyone else about your career goals and job search. You may discover a job opening that hasn't even been advertised yet!

You never know who may know about a job in retailing you're perfect for, or who may know someone who works at a store where you'd love to work. Only about 20 to 30% of job vacancies are advertised; many employers, especially small companies, prefer to look for employees by word of mouth. And remember, over 90% of all retailers are small employers.

"When you are looking to find a job within a particular company, your objective should be: Who do I know that might be able to make an introduction for me? As a first timer, this might be someone from school, church, your neighborhood, a relative, and so on" advises Tom Russell.

You can also make "blind contacts" at organizations to find knowledgeable and helpful people who can lead you to companies that are hiring. Look at Appendix A for a list of retail industry trade and professional associations. By contacting an organization in a retail sector (or niche) that interests you (for example, women's apparel, home furnishings, or electronics), you can gather much useful information about industry trends and employers. In addition, Appendix B describes some useful retailing books and industry magazines that can give you lots of insights into a retail career, as well as names of potential contacts. Finally, read on in this chapter for a sample "blind" cover letter to seek information about employment opportunities with a particular company that you've targeted.

Making Contact

In establishing networking contacts, be positive and enthusiastic. Remember, you are selling yourself! Use posture, words, expression, tone of voice to let them know this is a search you're excited about. And never act as if you don't deserve their time and help.

Introduce yourself to the contact, and tell him who gave you his name. Chat about "good old what's-his-name" (the person who referred you to the contact) briefly, if he wants to; remember, say only positive things! Say you're looking for a new job and would appreciate his advice. Arrange a good time to chat over the phone or to meet face to face.

> ### Networking with a Friend or with Anyone Who Knows You/Your Skills Well
>
> * Ask her to critique your strengths and weaknesses, and to give you advice on work settings or companies where she thinks you'd fit in well, and those to avoid.
>
> * Ask if she knows, or knows about, anyone who used to work or who currently works at any retail establishments that might have openings now or in the future.
>
> * If she doesn't know anyone like that, ask if she can think of anyone with a job history, skills, or interests similar to yours, who might be able to clue you into trends or job openings.
>
> * If she needs time to think about it, find out when you can contact her again to get the information.
>
> * Agree to show her your resume *if* she asks for it and if she's willing to show it to people who might be interested in you. You don't want her to throw your resume out or lose it in a drawer. If you're unsure what she'll do with your resume, it's better to explain you're planning to target your resume for specific companies/job openings, so anything you'd be able to give her would be very general.
>
> * For any names she gives you, get the proper spelling, learn whether the person is male or female, what his or her title is, and the phone number. If she gives you the phone number, find out if it's the person's home or work number.
>
> * For any names she gives you, get her permission to use her name as a referral source when you follow up on leads. If you don't get it, try to find out why.
>
> * Ask to keep in touch with her from time to time in case she hears of anything new. Make sure she has your phone number (and fax number, as appropriate) if she hears of anything in the meantime.
>
> * Thank her for her time. Thank her for any advice, information, or ideas she's given you. Thank her for her encouragement, support, and so on. Tell her you'll let her know when you've landed the new job.
>
> * After the discussion, send a thank-you note. Write it promptly! Make sure her name, title, and address, are absolutely correct. Be specific about how she's helped you move ahead in your job search. Enclose your resume only if she has agreed ahead of time to review it, and if you want her to do this.

Expanding Your Contacts

Ask the people you contact for the names of referrals. If appropriate, see if your contact (for example, your school's job placement specialist) would like to call the referral to prepare them for your call and make sure they're willing to talk with you.

Networking with a Potential Lead

- Send your resume to the person in advance of your conversation if there's time.

- Explain why you're contacting him.

- Summarize your background, special skills, and job goals.

- Let him know that you're looking for job leads, but you'd also appreciate any other pertinent advice, such as information about trends in your field, tips on upgrading your skills, or a constructive critique of your resume.

- If he is open to talking about job leads, find out if he, or his company, could use a person with your background or skills, or if he knows of someone who might.

- If he doesn't think he could use someone with your qualifications or really isn't aware of openings, ask if he can think of anyone else, either in his organization or in another, who might be able to clue you in to trends or job openings.

- If he needs time to think about it, find out when you can contact him again to get the information.

- For any names he gives you, get the proper spelling of the name, whether the person is male or female (if you aren't sure), any professional title like Dr., what his or her job is, and the phone number. If he gives you the phone number, find out if it's the person's home or work number.

- Find out, tactfully, what he knows (or has heard about) the lead.

- For any names he gives you, get his permission to use his name as a referral source when you follow up on his leads. If you don't get it, try to find out why.

- If this is a person you're willing to talk to again, ask his permission for you to keep in touch with him from time to time in case he hears of anything new. Make sure he has your phone number (and fax number, as appropriate) if he hears of anything in the meantime.

- Thank him for his time, as well as for any ideas, advice, information, encouragement, support, etc., he's given you. Tell him you'll let him know when you've landed the new job and you're back on "solid ground" again.

- After the discussion, send a thank-you note. Write it promptly! (Make sure his name, title, and address, etc., are absolutely correct!) Be specific about how he's helped you move ahead in your job search. Enclose your resume only if he has agreed ahead of time to review it.

Organizing Contacts

You'll need to keep tract of your contacts. Use a method that is comfortable and affordable for you. You might want to use a file box with 3 x 5 index cards, a notebook or personal "day planner" organizer, or even enter your contact data in a computer database. You may keep a file containing the business cards of contacts that you collect during your research, as appropriate.

Set up your "networking" file to include the following information about your contact:

- name (remember to include whether the person has a special title, such as "Dr." or "Reverend."
- address and telephone number (include an e-mail address if you have access to the Internet, or a fax number if you need it); note if these are for home or at work
- job title
- organization
- name of the person who referred you, or other information describing how you met this person
- date last contacted
- date you gave her your resume, if applicable
- summary of information, advice, or referrals she gave you
- names of referrals
- date you sent your thank-you note
- date for follow-up contact, if applicable
- other comments

Maintaining Contacts

A network is a dynamic thing, and to keep it useful you should stay in touch periodically with your contacts. Remember, most people don't stay in a single job forever, and you may need to contact someone in your network in the future. Therefore, it makes sense to keep in touch.

Check in with your retailing career-planning contacts every month or so while you're looking, to let them know how your training is going or how the job hunt progresses. If you land a good position in less time, alert your network about the good news once you've got your feet on the ground at work—say, after about three weeks on the job. If you're still looking or still in school, keeping visible may generate additional job leads.

In addition to sending thank-you notes, you can clip and send relevant articles or follow up on other information you come across that you believe may interest your contact. For example, if you and your contact talked about on-line shopping, fashion trends, or even hobbies and personal interests, mentioning these things in your follow-ups will make you stand out in her memory.

The Informational Interview

An *informational interview* is a great networking tactic. Informational interviewing can be extremely helpful in researching information about jobs, companies and schools.

When you do an informational interview, you are *not* asking for a job. Therefore, you don't need to be nervous about your interview. *You* will be asking the questions to find out what *you* want to know.

Informational interviews can be as casual as chatting with a sales associate at a store. Ask questions like, How many hours are you working? Do you have a future here? Do you like working here? What's the management like? What training do they give employees? Try to get detailed answers so you can find out if you'd like working there.

Most information interviews are more formal than talking with a person by the cash register. However you approach the interview, make a list of questions you want to ask the person you are interviewing. You can take your notes with you, and write down any information they tell you that you want to remember. After your appointment, be sure and send them a thank-you note.

Use the questions below as a guide. You may not need all of these; you may need to compose questions of your own to fit the circumstances of your information search. Where you read "this occupation/organization" below, substitute the names of the actual companies or specific fields you're researching in your question.

1. How did you get into this occupation/organization?
2. What attracted you to this career/organization?
3. How does someone interested in this field/organization progress from one job to the next?
4. What duties and responsibilities do you have in your job?
5. What skills or characteristics are needed to be successful in this career/organization?
6. What products or services do you (does this organization) make or provide, and who are the customers you serve? Who are your competitors? How does this firm rank against its competitors?

7. What preparation, education, training, or background does someone need to qualify for this job/organization?

8. What do you like/dislike about this career/organization? What are the major frustrations or annoyances in the occupation/organization?

9. What are the values and culture like here? What is the guiding philosophy of this organization?

10. What personality characteristics or attributes are important for someone who wants to succeed in this occupation/organization?

11. How much time does one need to devote in a week to be successful in this occupation/organization?

12. What are the beginning, average, and top salaries in this occupation? How does your organization pay in comparison to other organizations in the same industry? What fringe benefits are offered? (*Do not ask:* What is your salary?)

13. What opportunities exist for advancement, promotion, or change of jobs within the organization?

14. Could you suggest any temporary, part-time, or summer work experiences that would help me get ready for this career?

15. What school or college courses would you recommend to prepare for this occupation?

16. What other advice or information can you give to a person preparing to enter this occupation/organization? Because you know this occupation/organization better than I do, what other questions should I be asking about it?

17. May I contact you again if I need more information in the future?

18. Could you give me the names of other people I could talk to in this field/organization? May I mention your name as the person who referred me? Would you be willing to write a letter of introduction or introduce me over the phone?

RESUMES AND COVER LETTERS

Resumes and cover letters are ways to advertise yourself to potential employers. Many people don't use them to find their first job in retailing, but people who do will make a good first impression on employers. Make sure that your first impression is a positive one!

Writing Your Cover Letter

A cover letter introduces you and your resume to a potential employer. A good cover letter is neat, brief, and to the point. It is written with proper grammar, sentence structure, and punctuation. It contains *no* spelling or typographical errors.

Send the cover letter to a specific person, such as the company personnel manager or the manager you want to work for. If you don't know to whom you should write, the address, how to spell his name, or his job title, call the company and ask for this information. For instance, tell the receptionist, "I am calling to inquire where I should send my resume concerning jobs in sales (or in response to the ad that appeared in yesterday's classified ads, or whatever fits the circumstance). Can you tell me who that is, and how to spell his name (what his job title is, etc.)?"

The Cover Letter Formula

You have a maximum of 20 to 30 seconds to impress the reader with your letter, so make it clear, concise, and memorable. Try the following four-paragraph formula, but keep in mind that your letter is unique and specific to you. Don't make it look like a letter that any applicant could have written. Remember to use action verbs and the active voice.

- **First Paragraph:** Explain why you are writing, in such a way as to arouse the employer's interest. Hint: speak to your strengths.
- **Second Paragraph:** Briefly describe your professional and/or academic qualifications. Hint: If responding to a want ad, tailor this paragraph to the needs described in the ad.
- **Third Paragraph:** Relate yourself to the company, giving details as to why you should be considered. Do your homework—show that you know something about the organization. Hint: Don't ask what the employer can do for you; tell him or her what you can do for the company!
- **Fourth Paragraph:** Request action. Ask for an interview appointment—and then follow up. Be assertive; this is no time to leave the ball in the employer's court. Hint: Follow-up is key, so plan on making some phone calls.

Look at the sample cover letters that follow on the next few pages to get an idea how to tailor your cover letter to different circumstances.

Your Resume

A good resume will outline your education, work experience, special abilities, skills, and other pertinent information that describe you as the best-qualified candidate for a job. Still, no resume by itself ever earned anyone any job, anywhere. Resumes are designed to capture a potential employer's interest enough so that they will want to interview you. A good resume helps the employer predict how well you might perform in that desired future job, and how well you may fit within the company's style and philosophy. A resume may not be required for getting a position in retail, but it can help you more than you may think.

In a resume, you want to include the following information:

- career objective
- education
- work experience and employment history
- special skills
- other qualifications

Recent College Graduate Letter

Jane Smith
2557 Rosebud Way
Eugene, OR 97401
541-555-0303

June 17, 1998

John Waters
President
The California Look, Inc.
258 Sacramento Street
San Francisco, CA 94102

Dear Mr. Waters,

My outgoing personality, my sales experience, and my recent bachelor's degree in fashion merchandising make me a strong candidate for a position as a buyer for The California Look, Inc.

At Oregon State University I was president of both the Future Business Leaders of America and the American Marketing Association. Although a recent graduate, I am not a typical new graduate. As my enclosed resume illustrates, I've gained experience throughout college by working as a sales associate and assistant buyer for several shops in Oregon and Washington. These experiences have enhanced my formal education.

I have the maturity, skills, and abilities to embark on a career with The California Look, one of the fastest-growing women's apparel chains in the United States.

I will be in San Francisco at the end of this month, and I'd like very much to talk with you concerning a position with you. I will follow up this letter with a phone call to see if I can arrange a time to meet with you.

Thank you for your time and consideration.

Sincerely,

Jane Smith
Enclosure

Referral Cover Letter

Peter Brown
110 First Street
Alexandria, VA 22306
(802) 555-5544

April 15, 1998

Henrietta Garcia
Director of Human Resources
Best Shoes, Inc.
800 Madison Avenue
Suite 1209
New York, NY 10022

Dear Ms. Garcia,

Nancy Jones of Greenblatt & Associates, Inc. suggested I contact you regarding possible retail management openings in your firm. My resume is enclosed for your review.

As a shift supervisor at Luigi's, Alexandria's most exclusive men's apparel store, I've developed my talent and experience as a manager. Because the staff is very small, I've bought merchandise, developed advertising campaigns, and hired and trained sales associates. In the past year, I've been promoted twice.

Prior to my current position, I worked for Jones & Jones Marketing in Wichita, Kansas, where I prepared press releases and media guides, as well as coordinated direct mail campaigns.

My employers recognized my high degree of motivation and passion for retailing. They frequently added responsibility and accountability as I demonstrated my potential.

I am eager to talk with you about the contribution I could make to your firm. I will call you the week of April 25th to see if we can find a mutually convenient time and date to get together and discuss the possibility.

I greatly appreciate your consideration and look forward to meeting you soon.

Cordially,

Peter Brown

Enclosure

Cold Contact Cover Letter

Dana Baumgarten
1515 Oak Glen Way
P.O. Box 211
Belleview, NJ 08502
(908) 555-7495

October 12, 1998

Kristin Heller-Anderson
Manager, Collegiate Recruiting
Retail Pacesetters Corporation
One Retail Court
Trenton, NJ 08540

Dear Ms. Heller-Anderson,

Through my retail sales experiences throughout high school and college, and my capstone project at Trenton City College, I have learned a great deal about Retail Pacesetters and would like the opportunity to join such a dynamic organization as a management trainee.

I will be completing my Associate in Applied Science in Marketing degree in December and would be available to join a management training class in January.

I have proven my sales and customer service abilities by winning several sales competitions and quality service awards while employed part-time by Happy-Land Toys in the Trenton Mall for the past three years.

I will call you next week to discuss an interview. Thank you for your time and consideration.

Sincerely,

Dana Baumgarten

Enclosure

Classified Ad Response Cover Letter

Clark J. Michaels, Jr.
20651 West Peachtree Grove Lane, #204
Atlanta, GA 30303
(404) 555-3030

Judd Sumner
Store Manager
Allison's Hardware
22 Martin Luther King, Jr. Blvd.
Atlanta, GA 30308

Dear Mr. Sumner,

I believe I am the "multi-talented sales associate" you describe in your classified advertisement in today's Journal-Constitution. I'm a versatile and high-energy individual, and can start working evenings and weekends, if necessary, as early as next week.

Although I have been attending school full time as the enclosed resume shows, I shop regularly in Allison's when working on projects around the house and for my neighbors. I am impressed with the knowledge and gracious attitude with which I am always treated there. I am familiar with the range of products Allison's sells, and feel I represent the kind of do-it-yourself customer who loves to shop there.

I love tools and working with my hands. I am strong and ready to work hard. I have excellent communication and computational skills, am a team player, and have an excellent memory for names and faces.

I am a senior at Parks Senior High School. Dr. Jones, the principal, will provide a good reference. In fact, she's encouraging me to apply to Emory University to study business, since my goal is to own my own firm some day.

I will call you early next week. Please feel free to call me at the number above, or e-mail me at toolmancj@atlnet.com.

Thank you most sincerely for your time and consideration.

Very Truly Yours,

CJ Michaels

Enclosure

Top quality appearance in your resume is important. It showcases your qualifications and worth as a potential employee. Plan to spend considerable time preparing your resume. Develop it over time to allow consideration of information not immediately recalled. Never create a resume at the last minute; if you do, you're more likely to omit important information or produce a sloppy final product.

Develop a "self-inventory" of your background and qualifications, using the categories listed above, before writing the actual resume you'll provide to employers. This approach will help you prepare your "targeted" resumes. The targeted resume is customized to attract a specific employer's attention and make your resume stand out among the many they may receive from prospective employees. Then, when you sit down to create a resume targeted to respond to a want ad or based on what you've learned through your research and networking about that company, you can decide what elements from your inventory you want to include, and what elements you want to leave out.

A self-inventory can be created using index cards, using computer word-processing or database software, written in long-hand, or typed. By using smaller "bits" of information kept in a file or folder, you can keep updating information about you and organize the information in different ways, so that your resume always includes the most current information about you and presents it to employers in the most appealing ways.

Objective

The "objective" describes your reason for contacting the employer. You should be able to state your objective in about five or six words. Yana Parker, author of *The Damn Good Resume Guide*, says that "anything beyond that is probably 'fluff' and indicates a lack of clarity and direction."

Educational Background

When listing your educational background, start with your most recent training and proceed backward. Employers are looking for your most advanced qualifications at a glance. Include dates attended (or date you earned a diploma or degree), and name and location of school. If you have earned a college degree, you can omit your high school education.

Work Experience and Employment History

The key here is to list experiences (including, where applicable, relevant volunteer work) that relate to your job objective; highlight experiences where you applied skills that you can offer a new employer. For example, if you worked as a crew leader at a fast food restaurant, this would illustrate that you have teamwork and leadership skills, as well as experience interacting with the public—qualities that are important in any sales associate position. Likewise, if you were responsible for keeping the books for a club or for paying your family's bills, you will show how you have experience handling money. You also should include military service in this section.

Special Skills

List any skills, such as fluency in a foreign language, operating a cash register or computer, supervisory experience, and any other abilities that may be useful in your future job.

Other Qualifications

Other qualifications that appeal to employers may include leadership roles and participation in a community organization, or hobbies that would apply to a specific business—such as athletics, if you are applying to work in a sporting goods store, or refinishing antiques if you are applying to work in a furniture store. Think about your particular skills and how to present them in the best light.

About References

Some people include a line that says "References available (or provided) upon request" at the end of their resume. References are people who can honestly vouch for your skills, experience, and character to employers. Feel free to include this line if there's room on your resume, but don't force it on a one-page resume or add an extra sheet of paper just for this. You can include this information as part of your cover letter, or provide a list of references on a separate page with name, title, address, and phone number. Always get permission before you list anyone as a reference.

What to Leave Out of a Resume

Leave out anything that would not relate to your job performance. These include facts such as a disability, marital status, religion, age, weight, and so on. Do not include salary requirements, test results, or photographs.

Writing Your Resume

There are two ways to prepare a resume: the *functional* (or *skills*) resume, and the *chronological* resume. Some resumes combine these two approaches. Each strategy offers specific ways to highlight your strengths and to present your qualifications in the most appropriate light.

The Functional Resume

This type of resume emphasizes what you can do rather than what positions you have held. A skills-oriented format shows off your transferable skills (those that you can apply in any job, such as problem-solving ability, creativity, etc.) and takes the focus off your old job titles. This is a good approach if you have large gaps in your work history, if you haven't worked much (because you attended school full time, were a full-time homemaker, and so forth), or if you have skills that might be overlooked in a chronological resume.

Format for Functional Resume

NAME
Mailing Address
City, State, Zip Code
(Area Code) Phone Number
(Area Code) Fax Number if available
E-Mail address if used

OBJECTIVE: Briefly describe immediate and possible long range career goals.

SKILLS: (Subheadings may include: Interpersonal, Technical, Computer, Retail, etc.)

EDUCATION:
Institution, address (city and state).
Degrees in reverse chronological order. Date granted.
GPA-if applicable and complimentary.

Coursework (if applicable)

WORK EXPERIENCE:
(Subheadings may be: Professional Experience, Other Work Experience.)
Position title, where, and when.
Include full-time, part-time, related volunteer work, internships,and practical experience.

ACTIVITIES:
Indicate responsibilities, positions of leadership, and offices held.
Community and campus activities may be included.

HONORS:
List academic, leadership, athletic awards, scholarships, and memberships in honorary organizations.

HOBBIES:
List only if applicable to the organization or position.

REFERENCES:

The Chronological Resume

In this format, you summarize your work experience year by year. Begin with your current or most recent employer and work backward. For each position, list the name and location of the organization, the position you held, and pertinent dates. If you held the job for less than one year, include the months (such as January to May) as well as the year. Note which, if any, jobs were part-time. The chronological resume is appropriate for anyone with a fairly long work history using skills that relate to the job being sought.

Format for Chronological Resume

NAME
Mailing Address
City, State, Zip Code
(Area Code) Phone Number
(Area Code) Fax Number if available
E-Mail address if applicable

OBJECTIVE: Briefly describe immediate and possible long range career goals.

EDUCATION:
Institution, address (city and state).
Degrees in reverse chronological order. Date granted.
GPA-if applicable and complimentary.

Coursework (if applicable)

WORK EXPERIENCE:
(Subheadings may be: Professional Experience, Other Work Experience.)
Position title, where, and when.
Include full-time, part-time, related volunteer work, internships and practical experience.

SKILLS:
Include certifications, languages, technical/computer skills, etc.

ACTIVITIES:
Indicate responsibilities, positions of leadership, and offices held.
Community and campus activities may be included.

HONORS:
List academic, leadership, athletic awards, scholarships, and memberships in honorary organizations.

HOBBIES:
List only if applicable to the organization or position.

REFERENCES:

Other Resume Tips

Resumes should be easy to read. Use white, cream, or light gray paper; these leave the most professional impression. Remember to type your resume. If you use a computer, use easy-to-read fonts, such as Times, Garamond, and Arial. Careful use of all capital letters, bold print, and underlining will call attention to headings and important information. Be consistent and conservative in using different fonts, font sizes, or styles. Use two fonts, three at most. For example, use **Arial Bold 14** for headings, *Arial Italic 12* for subheadings, and Times New Roman 11 for text.

Organize the resume so that the most important information appears near to the top of the page. Structure the sections within your resume to reflect this. The first thing the reader will see is your name, address, and phone number, followed by objective. After that, arrange your sections to highlight what the employer wants to see first, second, third, and so on. This means, for example, that if your work experience is more relevant to the position you're applying for than your education, the section on work experience should be placed above your education section.

Type or print your resume on good quality 8 1/2 x 11 paper. Resumes should contain *no* spelling or typographical errors, and should have a consistent style. Have a couple of people proofread your resume to make sure that there are no errors. One-page resumes are best, but two-page resumes are appropriate if needed.

Never crowd the page with too much information, and there should be plenty of "white space"—wide margins, and ample space between categories to place emphasis on specific data. The resume should be easy for employers to scan; in fact, some experts believe it should take no longer to get the key points from a resume than the time it takes for a sheet of paper to travel from the desk to the wastepaper basket. That may be an exaggeration, but you get the idea; make your resume concise enough to impress the employer with your qualifications in less than a minute, tops!

Full sentences are not necessary when writing a resume; in fact, avoid using pronouns (*I, me, they*, etc.), or helping verbs such as *am, did, was*, and the like. Instead, use short phrases with attention to clarity of meaning. Use the present tense to denote current activities, past tense for past activities. Emphasize accomplishments and problem-solving skills, not merely duties or responsibilities. Highlight your leadership potential, organizational ability, communication skills, ingenuity, and teamwork.

Start lines with verbs (for example, *managed*, *operated*, or *produced*) to describe your accomplishments and abilities. See the box describing "Action Verbs" for more tips on ways to describe your skills and responsibilities.

Sample Action Verbs

Action verbs verbs give your resume power and direction. Try to begin all "skills" statements with an action verb. Here is a sample of action verbs for different types of skills:

Management skills: administered, analyzed, coordinated, developed, directed, trained, evaluated, improved, supervised

Technical skills: assembled, built, calculated, designed, operated, overhauled, remodeled, repaired, programmed

Clerical skills: arranged, catalogued, compiled, generated, organized, processed, systematized

Creative skills: conceptualized, created, designed, established, fashioned, illustrated, invented, performed

Financial skills: administered, analyzed, balanced, budgeted, forecast, planned, projected

Helping skills: assessed, coached, counseled, diagnosed, facilitated, represented

Research Skills: clarified, evaluated, identified, inspected, organized, summarized

Communications skills: arranged, addressed, authored, drafted, formulated, persuaded, explained

Miscellaneous retail skills: sold, marketed, advertised, served, wrapped, totaled, displayed, arranged, stocked

---

Your local library, career center, or bookstore should carry books with sample resumes for you to review. See Appendix B (Additional Resources) for some suggested reading.

Here are some sample resumes, in the chronological, functional, and combination (chronological-functional) format.

Sample Chronological Resume

Robin Brennan
2274 Bluebird Ct.
Springfield, OH 81506
(937) 555-3341
robbie@gj1.com

OBJECTIVE: Assistant buyer

EDUCATION: Bowling Green State University
                                  Bowling Green, Ohio
                                  1996 Bachelor of Arts, Fashion Merchandising

Academic Honors   Phi Upsilon Omicron—the National Honor Society of
                                       Home Economics
                                  Dean's List, Fall 1994

Activities   Fashion Merchandising Association—3 years:
                                  Vice President, 1996
                                  Chair, Executive Planning Committee, 1995
                                  Chair, Fundraising and Membership Committee, 1994

                                  Secret Shopper in a Fashion Merchandising class

EMPLOYMENT:
7/97–present   Too Fine!
part-time   Springfield, OH
                                  Sales Associate/Assistant Buyer

                                  Provide customer service
                                  Open and close the store
                                  Manage girl's and excess merchandise
                                  Execute window changes and floor sets

12/96–7/97   Maurice's
part-time   Springfield, OH
                                  Sales Associate

                                  Provided customer service
                                  Sized and straightened merchandise
                                  Executed floor moves
                                  Kept layaways current

11/95–8/96   JC Penney Co.
part-time   Bowling Green, OH
                                  Sales Associate, Ladies Sportswear

                                  Provided customer service
                                  Sized and straightened sections
                                  Executed floor changes

5/94–7/97   National City Bank
summers and holidays   Springfield, OH
                                  Customer Service Representative

                                  Performed transactions
                                  Filed signature cards
                                  Answered phones

References available upon request.

Sample Functional Resume

LEE ALBRIGHT
123 Lincoln Street #110
Portland, ME 18512
(207) 555-5372

OBJECTIVE
An assistant manager position in a progressive retail company

HIGHLIGHTS OF QUALIFICATIONS
Three years experience in retail industry
Marketing and sales of various products
Experience in supervising and training employees
Computer skills
Strong oral and written communication skills

CAREER RELATED EXPERIENCE

Management

- Assisted in the management of retail store operations
- Supervised and trained seven new employees
- Gained experience in inventory control, pricing, customer service

Marketing

- Earned sales award for exceeding sales quotas
- Suggested, designed, and implemented successful promotional event
- Arranged merchandise displays

Additional Skills

- Handling cash and credit transactions
- Departmental bookkeeping
- Word Perfect, Lotus 1-2-3, dBase experience

EMPLOYMENT

1995-present   Sales Associate (part-time), Wal-Mart, Orono, ME

1991-1995   Cashier (part-time), Portland Convention Center, Portland, ME

EDUCATION   University of Maine, Orono
B.S. cum laude, Business Management, May 1998
Cumulative Grade Point Average 3.70 (4.0 Index)
                Down East Community College, Portland ME
A.A. Communications, June 1994
Cumulative Grade Point Average 3.2 (4.0 index)

References provided upon request

Sample Combination resume

Shelby Lee
4410 Washington Drive
Norfolk, Virginia 33333
(757) 555-1234
e-mail: shelby_lee@commonwealth.net

Objective: Retail sales, leading to management opportunities

QUALIFICATIONS BRIEF
Excellent interpersonal and customer service skills, patient and effective when working with a wide range of personalities
Accomplished problem-solver in retail environments
Successful in learning and comprehending new systems and methods

RELEVANT SKILLS AND ACCOMPLISHMENTS
Financial Skills:
Reconciled cash records to computer records for over 200 accounts on a monthly basis.
Prepared monthly payroll, paid bills, and processed tuition payments for a co-op day care center/preschool.

Supervisory Skills:
Trained nine sales associates, most of whom had no prior experience, in customer service and store operations.
Wrote a Product Knowledge pamphlet, minimizing training time for new employees.
Maintained cordial working relationships while explaining and clarifying errors.
Interviewed and hired four staff members.

Computer Skills:
Worked with software vendor in development of specialty reports.
Assisted in implementation of new POS program.
Input monthly account records on a PC.

Problem Solving Skills:
Designed a coding system to eliminate dual product coding and time wasting correlating sales reports.
Coordinated return and exchange of recalled products.
Reviewed company procedures, identifying sources of high error frequency; recommended revisions adopted by management, resulting in 14% fewer errors over three quarters.

EMPLOYMENT HISTORY
1996-98 Treasurer/Bookkeeper (20 hours/month)
Little Harvard Children's Center. Hidden Hills, VA

1994–98 Senior Sales Associate, Gifts
Jonson's Department Store, Alexandria, VA

1990–94 Quartermaster Specialist 1st Class
United States Air Force, stationed in the US and Korea

EDUCATION
B.A. in Communicatons, minor in Accounting & Business
Norwest College, Berkeley, Calif.

A Word about Scannable Resumes

Many corporations are now electronically scanning paper-based resumes into computerized databases. Before you send a copy of your resume to a company, contact them by phone and ask whether they scan incoming resumes. Yana Parker suggests if they do, you may could send two copies—one to be read by human being, one to be electronically read by the scanner. "*Make sure* you identify which resume is for what purpose," she warns. You can attach a sticky note for this purpose.

For a Resume the Scanner Likes:

* Use text only, and no fancy fonts, underlining, bold or italic text, etc. Parker recommends clear fonts such as Times, Palatino, Arial, Universal, Helvetica, or Bookman.
* Use *job-specific key words*. Industry terms, buzzwords, jargon; hard skills and commonly used trade terms are what the computer will look for. If you do not know what those terms are for your desired job, find out. (Informational interviewing is a very effective way to get that information.)
* Print your resume on a high-resolution laser printer.
* Send an original resume, not a photocopy. The clearer the copy, the better job the scanner can do.

What if You Have Gaps in Your Work History?

Yana Parker encourages anyone who has been doing other things besides working (or attending school, fulfilling military service, performing community service, etc.) to look at your chronological history in a different light. She says, "Tell what you *were* doing, as gracefully as possible—rather than leaving a gap. If you were doing anything valuable (even if unpaid) during those so-called "gaps," you could just insert that into the work-history section of your resume to fill the hole."

For example, try this:

1993-95: Stay-at-Home Parent (or traveling, or caring for disabled relative, etc.)

What if Your Work History Includes Very Short-Time Jobs?

To minimize the job-hopper image, Parker recommends combining several similar jobs (even those separated by periods of time when you didn't work or held other kinds of jobs) into one "chunk," for example:

1993-1995 Cashier: Heavenly Bakery, United Multiplex Cinemas, Carter Drugs *or*

1996-98: Counter Person/Server: McDonald's Restaurant, Burger King, Tony's Pizza

Also, Parker says, "You can just drop some of the less important, briefest jobs. But don't drop a job, even when it lasted a short time, if that was where you acquired important skills or experience."

What If You Didn't Finish School?

If you left school before earning your diploma or finishing your degree, don't leave out the parts of your education you did complete. Include school names, dates, and locations, and emphasize what courses you did complete. You may want to note in your cover letter why you haven't earned your degree, such as "I am taking a break in my education to get practical work experience (and earn money to pay for tuition and books, etc.)."

Certainly, it never hurts to be honest if you've learned academics aren't for you. You can tell employers something like "I've discovered that working motivates me much more than studying. Although I hope to earn my degree in the future, right now I want to apply my energy and enthusiasm by working at a company like yours."

Ways to Impress an Employer in a Cover Letter and a Resume

Parker urges job-seekers to use "PAR" statements in a resume. These statements can also be extremely effective in a cover letter.

PAR stands for Problem-Action-Results. Here's how it works:

- First you state the problem that existed in your workplace (or in any situation where you solved a challenging problem)
- Second, you describe what action you took to resolve the problem.
- Third, specify the beneficial results of your action.
- Finally, rewrite the PAR statement to emphasize your action; communicate your statement in one sentence (two sentences at most in a cover letter).

Here's an example from a resume. Note there are no pronouns here; in a cover letter, you do need to use pronouns:

> "Transformed an inefficient sales force into a cohesive team by rescheduling hours to meet customer demands, and leading team meetings; this resulted in 12% greater sales and 25% less staff turnover in one year."

A Final Note about Resumes and Cover Letters

Never lie on your cover letter or your resume. Every interested employer should and will check into your background carefully; if you misrepresent yourself, you'll suffer more than the employer. Employers do not want to hire people they cannot trust.

Acing Your Interview

The interview is the most important aspect of any job hunt. The impression you make on the employer will likely be the reason you do or don't get a job offer.

Most people feel anxious about interviews, but preparing yourself in advance can lower your stress level, and will help you perform better during the process.

Preparing for the Interview

Before going to the interview, you should research the company to learn as much as you can; this information will enable you to demonstrate your knowledge and interest during the interview. Ask the reference librarian at your local library to help you find what's published about the organization. Search for information about the company on the Internet, if you can. You can even contact the company directly in advance of the interview and see if they have any brochures, press releases, or an annual report you can examine before your interview.

Make sure you go to the interview dressed well. What you wear says a tremendous amount about your personality and attitude. Remember, in retail you are representing the company to the public, so how you look is very important.

Is What You Wear Who You Are?

Marlow Hill manages the Retail Learning Center at the Louisiana Business Partnership in Baton Rouge. She trains job seekers and retail personnel to launch and enhance their careers. She describes the importance of appearance in retail:

"What a younger person may think of as 'cool' is different from what is 'business appropriate.' In my courses we'll go out to the mall and identify professional attire. We work with magazines to look at pictures that demonstrate what proper professional attire looks like. I took one young lady under my wing. She started as a freshman, dressed as a hippie. She had a pierced tongue, dark lipstick, nails and clothes, and dyed black hair. We stressed the importance of appearance in retailing—WE set the stage for our customers. The growth I saw was amazing. She came out of her cocoon and turned into a butterfly. She changed her clothing to softer colors and professional attire, changed her hair to a soft brown, and uses softer makeup. Her career is really taking off."

Leave enough time in your schedule to get to the interview site about 15 minutes early. This lets you find a place to park or walk from the bus stop to the company, find the office where the interview takes place, and visit the restroom as needed. Ensuring that you show up on time for your interview shows respect for the company and the interviewer. Always make sure that you allow extra time if you are unfamiliar with the employer's location.

In addition, allow at least two hours until your next appointment. That's not to say that all job interviews last a long time (although some employers want to spend the best part of a day with you, to have you meet a number of people, tour the facility, take pre-employment screening tests, and so forth); rather, it's a mistake to feel rushed or to leave the impression that you have more important things to do than participate in the interview.

Do's and Don'ts for the Interview

- Wear clothes like the people who work there. Retail professionals tend to dress professionally: men usually wear ties, and often a sports coat. They generally wear dress shoes. Women not only dress well, they always wear hosiery and dress shoes. Dress as though you are ready and enthusiastic to go to work. If you must wear earrings to the interview, wear the smallest ones you have. Go easy on the trendy make-up or hairstyles (anything that calls attention to how "out there" you look and takes away attention from your skills and qualifications), unless you want to work in a place where everyone—managers, employees, and customers alike—looks that way. Leave your hat at home.
- Go alone—don't bring a friend or relative. If someone takes you to the interview, leave them in the car or arrange to meet them after the interview.
- Be polite and show respect to everyone you meet, including the boss, the boss's secretary, and so on.
- Leave your problems at home. Focus on what you can offer the boss to address his or her problems; don't talk about how this job or this company can help you solve your problems.
- Catalogue your skills before going into the interview. Bring a list with you, as necessary. You acquire skills in many ways, and not just in the workplace. Babysitting, shopping and handling money, selling Girl Scout cookies or collecting tickets for the school play can lead to a career in retailing.

So can your interests or hobbies. Other skills you may already have include doing work around the house, using computers, volunteering in the community, or participating in school activities. Each time you do something new, each time you take on new responsibilities, you learn some skills, and those skills can get you a good career in retailing. Make sure you tell the boss what you have done and what you can do for him or her.

♦ Bring a fact sheet or resume with you. Even if the interviewer has a copy, another copy can be useful for you to refer to as you answer questions.

♦ Make hiring you the easiest decision an employer can make. Follow up with a thank-you note to the interviewer or a phone call to let them know you are interested.

Answering Tough Questions

Essentially, there are just three interview questions. All the other questions interviewers will ask you are designed to get enough information to answer these few questions.

The first question is, "Can you, and will you, do this job better than the other applicants, and will hiring you be better than not hiring anyone at all?"

The second question is, "Will you fit in with the rest of the people who work here?"

The third question is, "How much will it cost me (in terms of paying you, training you, supervising you, and so on) to employ you?" In retailing especially, another way of looking at this question is to say, "Will hiring you result in my company making more money than it costs to have you on staff?"

Now, it's unlikely that any interviewer will be so blunt as to ask you any of these three questions directly. If they did, most applicants would have a hard time answering them. Do you think you could answer these questions? What would you say?

Most interviewers enter the interview with a list of questions they have developed or that they have been directed to ask all applicants by the Human Resources department. These questions tend to be of two types: direct questions, such as "When can you start?" and open-ended questions, such as "What would you say are your greatest strengths?"

When responding to the interviewer's questions, think about what the interviewer really wants to know. Think of yourself as a product you want to sell to the employer. What are your features? For example, you offer excellent interpersonal skills, loyalty, enthusiasm, and a passion for helping people. How will your features benefit the employer? Using this example, your features mean you will do whatever it takes to satisfy your customers, work cooperatively with others, and help the company triumph over its competitors.

The Mock Job Interview

Consider enlisting help from a trusted friend, instructor, or family member to do a "mock" interview in advance of the real thing. Treat it as a "dress rehearsal," so prepare for it and make it as realistic as possible. Sit together in a quiet room, and don't allow yourselves to be distracted by the phone, other people, etc. During this trial run, the "interviewer" asks you key questions about you and the job you're seeking, and you answer them as truthfully as possible. Then, assess together how you did, and work on polishing the parts that didn't come out as well as you'd hoped.

Answer interview questions in terms of the job you are applying for, emphasizing experiences and qualities that make you the best candidate for the position. Note: if there is any question where the answer makes you appear less than qualified for the job, add something to the answer to indicate what you learned from your experience that will help you improve in the future.

Here are common open-ended interview questions. This is by no means a complete list, but it will give you an idea of what you can expect. As you read through them, make notes to yourself about how you might answer them briefly, concisely, honestly, and accurately.

- Tell me about yourself.
- What are your career objectives?
- Why should we hire you?
- What do you know about this company?
- Why do you want to work here?
- What are your strengths and weaknesses?
- Describe a situation in which you used your skills to solve a problem.
- Describe a situation in which you failed at something, and tell me what you learned from it.
- What kind of supervision do you work best under, and why?
- Why did you leave your last position?
- What was your favorite (or least favorite) position, and why?

- Tell me about your greatest accomplishments.
- What do you see yourself doing five (or ten, or two) years from now?

Asking Questions

Usually, the interviewer will invite you to ask questions toward the end of the interview. Always have some questions (three to five is a good number) to ask. This is a good way to set yourself above the rest of the pack of applicants. Asking well thought-out questions demonstrates that you have done your homework about the company and that you are as interested in finding out that you will fit in with them and achieve your career goals as they are in learning if you're the right person for the job.

You may not have as much time as you'd like to ask all your questions, so plan to ask the most important questions first.

Never, ever ask about salary, vacation, or other benefits during a job interview. Doing so communicates that you are only interested in what you are going to get out of the job. Remember, the point of the interview is to communicate what you have to offer the employer; that is, what *they* get from *you*. The time to talk about money and other goodies is after the employer has offered you the job.

Here is a list of appropriate questions to ask when the interviewer invites you. The interviewer's responses to your questions should, in turn, enable you to follow up with additional information about yourself. This will give you the opportunity to illustrate again that you are the best candidate for the job.

Select the questions that best fit your circumstances, or develop questions of your own.

- How do you evaluate employees and identify those who are ready for advancement?
- Describe what I would be doing during the first 30 (or 60, or 90) days (or first 6 months, or whatever) on the job.
- What kinds of challenges would I be facing on this job?
- Tell me about the people I would be working most closely with.
- How would you describe the company's strengths and weaknesses?
- How are "star" employees recognized in this company?
- What qualities are you looking for in the ideal candidate for this position?
- What kind of person is most likely to succeed in this company?

- How would you describe your management philosophy/style? (If the interview is with someone other than the person you would be working for, rephrase the question.)
- What kinds of things does this company do to develop employees?

Leave time to ask the following question. Employers are always impressed when you ask it, and you can get some useful information from their answers.

- If you were being interviewed for this position, knowing what you know about this company and this job, what questions would you be asking?

Follow-up Tactics

Within two or three days of the interview, send a thank-you note to the interviewer. Thank the employer for his or her time and interest in you, and mention important qualifications that you may have omitted during the interview, or any other important points discussed.

WHAT HAPPENS AFTER THE INTERVIEW?

It's not that common to receive a job offer at the interview, unless the employer is really desperate! The interviewer will usually review your interview, confer with his or her staff, or interview other applicants before making a decision and extending an offer.

Generally, a decision is made within a few weeks. If you don't hear from the employer within the time suggested during the interview, follow up with a courteous phone call, but don't become a pest by calling every day for an answer.

If you learn someone else got the job, it's appropriate to write a brief note thanking the company for the opportunity to interview for the company, and express your interest in continuing a dialogue with them to be considered for future opportunities.

When you are offered the job, decide how you are going to accept or decline (yes, you have that option!) the position. In some cases, you'll get an offer in writing; in others, the offer may be a verbal one. It's a good idea to send your answer in writing, even if you've already told the employer what you've decided in person or over the phone. In your acceptance letter, include the start date, agreed hourly wage or salary and any other pertinent information that clarifies the terms of the job. If you decline the offer, be gracious and consider leaving the door open by inviting the company to contact you in the event a more appropriate opportunity opens in the future.

A FINAL WORD

Don't get frustrated with the job hunt. Every day people retire or quit, and new businesses open. All these things create job opportunities in retailing. Congratulate yourself on your efforts, and remember that every step you take gets you closer to achieving your goal. You may have to look hard to get the job that's best for you, but it's out there!

THE INSIDE TRACK

Who:	Angélica Marquez
What::	Manager, Pine River Valley Collectibles (AKA Penny's Coffee House)
Where:	Ignacio, Colorado
Education:	High School Graduate, on-the-job training

Insider's Advice

No one ever told me I wasn't old enough or that I couldn't do anything. I started working here two years ago as a high school junior, as part of the School to Career program. At first, I ran the register and did customer service after school. I wasn't particular about what I would or wouldn't do. I did everything: mopping, customer service, cooking, whatever.

After three months the owner gave me a raise, and asked me to work full time in the summer. I opened the place by myself, had my own set of keys. I got the store ready before the owner came in. I recruited, hired, and trained my friends for summer work. I have excellent training and people skills. I have good instincts about people.

The best advertising is word of mouth from customers. Customer service is crucial. People expect service. People notice service; they aren't dumb. Keep your product quality and your service wonderful, and you'll be a success. You can't have a bad day; the unhappy customer will go to the next clerk, or go somewhere else. You have to consistently treat them all with a smile and courtesy. People will come to you when they know you give them what they want and treat them well.

Retail is all about commitment, energy, and focus. Teens need to be told that they can be an asset to the company. They need to prove they have goals, that they can do more than what's expected of them. They need someone to say, "I see something in you; I want you to work for me."

Insider's Take on the Future

My long-term goal is to operate my own catering business. The owner and her partner are expanding the place into a restaurant to my specifications. I'm organizing, and reading lots of books on hiring and management. I want to earn a degree in business or accounting, but not right away. I want to work, do what I like, take correspondence classes. Everything has worked out so great so far. I like [the town of] Ignacio. I like knowing everybody and calling them by their first name. I'm going to be really, really happy being where I am.

CHAPTER | 6

This chapter gives you useful information for thriving in your new retail career. You'll learn about managing work relationships, fitting in with the workplace culture, managing your time, finding a mentor, and promoting yourself from within. Also, you'll find advice about effective selling and customer service from retail managers and workers already in the field.

HOW TO SUCCEED ONCE YOU'VE LANDED THE JOB

Landing a job is one thing. Succeeding at the job is something else. After investing your time, money and energy in completing a training program and accepting a position, you need to work hard not only at fulfilling job duties and responsibilities, but also at managing your time and handling new relationships with your managers and coworkers. This chapter will show you how to make yourself a stand-out employee with excellent chances of advancing in your chosen career.

FITTING IN AT WORK

Fitting in at work is a lot like fitting in at school, finding your place in a new neighborhood or, if you're married, getting along with a new family. Many people feel anxious, eager to please, and to be accepted.

These feelings are normal and even helpful. Why? Because they make you pay careful attention to the signals you receive from the new people around you, and they help you learn and remember new rules, unfamiliar terms, and special ways of doing things. If you work hard to be accepted and believe in what your company and colleagues are doing, you'll feel comfortable and successful before you know it.

The retail industry is highly competitive. The retail work environment is goal-oriented, much like an athletic team. The goal is to beat the competition. Very seldom is there only one supplier (for any length of time, anyway) to the public of whatever it is that your company sells. In addition to competing against other retailers, in a friendly way, different stores in the same company compete with each other to make the most sales. Different departments in the same store compete to see who can make the most sales. Sales associates in the same department compete to make the most sales in the group. And the department competes with itself to outsell the same period last week or last year.

Here are some simple rules for being valuable to your employer and for being a team player:

- Be on time for work and meetings.
- Listen more than you talk.
- Follow guidelines for taking breaks and meals, using the telephone, appropriate work dress, and so on.
- Look and behave professionally at all times. Treat supervisors, coworkers, and customers with courtesy, honesty, and good humor. Make everyone glad to spend time with you.
- Limit how much personal information you share; it's not necessary to tell everyone your life story, or unload your personal problems on your supervisor. Keep your work life and your home life separate.
- Don't burn any bridges. You never know when you will have to work with someone again.
- Don't be a gossip.
- Be helpful. When other people on your team do well, so will you. Volunteer to take on assignments you're ready for. Be prepared to go the extra mile.
- Be thankful when people help you. In addition, celebrate others' accomplishments.
- When you have a problem affecting how well you do your job, go to your supervisor and discuss it. He or she will appreciate it if you come prepared with at least one alternative solution to the problem; this tells your boss

(and your coworkers) that you aren't a whiner, but do need his or her help in finding the best approach.

- If you have a communication problem with a coworker, try to work together to solve the problem before involving your supervisor.
- Accept responsibility. Don't take credit for others' ideas, and own up to your mistakes.
- Do what you promise to do; show others they can depend on you.
- Avoid blaming others. Try to see a conflict in terms of the situation and actions rather than personalities—you can work on changing the situation as much as possible, but it's unlikely you'll ever be able to change anyone's personality.

MANAGING WORK RELATIONSHIPS

There are three types of relationships in the work environment: how you relate with your customers, your coworkers, and your supervisors.

Managing Relationships With Your Customers

In retailing, no matter what your position, you'll be working in customer service. You'll be trying to help someone, whether your customer is a member of the public or another employee of your company.

When a customer needs you, often she is feeling anxious about something—she is looking for a specific item she must buy today, she is worried about missing a looming deadline, or something else that she feels she can't do without your help. If someone is vague, tense, or short with you, remember to look at the situation as an opportunity to help your customer solve a problem. Be empathetic; try putting yourself in your customer's shoes. Be friendly, and work with her to find just what she needs. If you do, she'll think well of you, and seek you out the next time.

Managing Relationships With Your Coworkers

Some people you work with will impress you; other won't. You'll get along with some colleagues, and some you'll wish you had never met. Regardless of the quality of the relationship, you will have to work together to help accomplish your company's aims.

Take advantage of company-sponsored training to understand more about personality styles, to learn to manage conflict better, or to improve your interpersonal skills. Learn about other departments and how each area works together. Exchanging information with colleagues in other areas will help you present your organization in a positive light to the public, make you more resourceful when providing effective customer service, and may help you become aware of job openings in other departments.

Managing Your Relationship with Your Boss(es)

With luck, you'll find your supervisor to be a mentor, a role model, and someone who will stand behind you to help you succeed in your company. But even if your boss is hard to please or get along with, as long as you work in the same company it pays to do your best to be friendly and to keep the lines of communication open.

Become familiar with your supervisor's management style and adjust yourself to work within that style. Find out what his or her expectations are for you. Find out what kind of decisions your boss permits you to make on your own, and what kind he or she expects you to bring to their attention.

Make sure you know what your boss's communication expectations are— meeting together periodically, working side by side, or only communicating when there's a problem to deal with. Explore your goals with your boss, and ask for his help in reaching them. In addition, try to discover your boss's career goals too; if you can help your supervisor achieve her goals, it can only make you look good as well.

COMMUNICATING: THE KEY TO SUCCESSFUL RELATIONSHIPS

Verbal and Nonverbal Communication

Words aren't the only way we communicate. Experts estimate that words deliver only 10 to 30% of our interpersonal communication! The rest is nonverbal. We send messages to others about our thoughts, feelings, and priorities through our appearance and dress, facial expressions, posture, gestures, and eye contact—even the way we decorate our office or workspace.

What are you telling your customers, your colleagues, or your boss by your nonverbal behavior? When we talk with someone we like and agree with, we often show it by:

- smiling (communicates "I enjoy your company")
- showing the palms of the hand (communicates "I'm open to you")

* head tilting (communicates "I'm interested in what you're saying")
* leaning forward (communicates "I'm interested in you")

When we're afraid of, dislike, or disagree strongly with someone, we may use our bodies to try to keep the person at a distance. These are some of the signs:

* body turned slightly away (communicates "I want to get away from you")
* crossed legs (usually communicates "I'm uncomfortable")
* arms crossed in front of chest (communicates "I'm afraid of you" or "I disagree with you")
* clenched hands (communicates "I'm afraid")
* tightly crossed ankles (communicates "I'm uncomfortable")
* hand on the back of the neck (communicates "you're a pain in the neck")
* upturned chin (communicates "I don't like you")

All of the following nonverbal behaviors communicate boredom:

* fidgeting
* drumming on table
* kicking motion
* vacant stare (not blinking much)
* head propped up on hand
* sighing

Your verbal communication often reflects your mood, too. What happens when you're feeling tense or anxious? Your may stammer, speak too quickly, say "uh" and "um" a lot, or lose your train of thought.

Tips for Improving Communication at Work

Although there are "official" rules that are written down, there are also codes that you just learn by experience. Most work communication rules are unspoken.

To be successful at work, keep these tips in mind:

* Say "I understand" if you're receiving instructions.
* Learn to speak your employer's language. Learn the company's unique terms, acronyms, and abbreviations and use them appropriately in conversations with your boss and coworkers.
* Follow the company's nonverbal communication rules. Follow the official or unofficial dress code. Keep your work space neat and organized.

- If you and your boss have problems communicating, study your boss's personality and preferences. Learn when and how to present information to the boss.

Tips for Communicating with Everyone

Here are guidelines for communicating better, wherever you go:

- Beware of distracting people when you communicate, especially in the work place. In *The Last Word on the Gentle Art of Verbal Self-Defense*, Suzette Haden Elgin warns against *twirks*. A twirk is a communication behavior that attracts attention to itself, and away from what you're saying. Twirks include some accents, using bad grammar, and cursing. It also refers to saying things like *you know, he goes, like,* and *okay* too often.

- Whenever you don't understand what someone means, ask for clarification. Try saying, "I'm afraid I don't follow you." Or, you can use a phrase like, "If I heard you correctly, you said/feel/want…" to paraphrase what you heard. Then say, "Is that right?"

- Don't whine.

- Be polite. Someone else's rudeness doesn't give you the right to be rude in return.

- Substitute negative or pessimistic words like *hard, tough* and *impossible* with productive ones like *interesting* or *challenging.*

- Listen. During a conversation, acknowledge what the other person says or feels. Using phrases like "I see you're upset" or "You have a point" doesn't mean you agree with what they say or feel; it's a way to confirm that you are listening to their point of view.

- Learn to respond as well as to listen. Come forward when you're annoyed or upset. No one can read your mind. Use "I" messages; for example, tell your coworker, "I'm angry that you didn't let me know that you expected me to cover for you this morning. That left us short, and we had some unhappy customers as a result."

- During a disagreement, try to work out a compromise. Engage in give-and-take and come to an agreement both sides can live with.

- Don't be bossy, especially if you're not the boss. Avoid telling people they "should do such and such" or "should have done such and such."

- Be sure you can take criticism yourself. Be willing to admit when you've made a mistake.

THE WORKPLACE CULTURE

Some retail workplaces are formal, suit-and-tie environments. Others are laid back and casual. Most lie somewhere in between. Let's look at the three basic types of retail cultures. Think of them as benchmarks on a continuum of work environments; remember that the company you work for may share attributes of each, and these qualities may overlap or even conflict with one another.

The Entrepreneurial Culture

This type of organization emphasizes risk-taking and independence. These companies move fast to stay on top of the competition. They keep their products and services on the cutting edge of their market. They often pay their sales force on commission.

The Small-Business Culture

This type is more relaxed than the often stressful, fast-paced entrepreneurial culture. Retail companies with this type of culture are willing to take risks, but usually after more careful thought, brainstorming, and evaluation. This environment values cooperation and shared growth. This means that if one person (one department, one branch, etc.) does well, everyone else shares in the benefits. Not all companies with this type of culture are small, and not all small companies have adopted this culture.

The Corporate Culture

This is a hierarchical organization that tends to have many layers of reporting and management: imagine the "chain of command" used in the military. Retail organizations with thousands of employees and many facilities often adopt this style because it streamlines certain kinds of communication. In this system, salaries and other employee benefits are usually stratified and formalized; there are often more "rules" than in the other two types.

Getting Along in Your Company Culture

Getting along in your company's culture means that you must figure out what it's like, and how that jives with your own style as a worker. If you're anxious to make your mark quickly and rise to the top, a company that leans toward the entrepreneurial end of the continuum may be the best fit. If you are less interested in internal competition, a small-business culture may suit you better. And if you feel you want to follow a stable, predictable timetable and have a very clear sense of where the boundaries are in an organization, a corporate culture might feel right. You may be surprised where you fit, and as you grow and develop your skills and experiences in retailing, your comfort level may shift.

TIME MANAGEMENT

No matter what the workplace culture is like, the typical retail environment is hectic. Working evenings, weekends, and holidays is standard for anyone having contact with the public—from the company president to the most junior sales associate. Anyone working on a management track in retail is bound to work over 60 hours every week for years. People with a passion for retail know this, expect it, and thrive in this type of environment.

How do retailing professionals deal with these demands on their time? Here are some keys:

+ Know your job. Know what you are expected to do, what results your boss expects you to deliver, on a daily, weekly, or monthly basis. Discuss issues that may conflict with fulfilling these obligations as soon as you become aware of them.

+ Prioritize and organize, with your manager's help as needed. All career retailers juggle multiple tasks simultaneously; that's part of the fun of the work—it's rarely boring! But make sure you put your time and energy where it's needed, and avoid procrastinating, outside distractions, and time-wasting activities.

+ Use daily or weekly planners religiously to make lists and jot down your commitments. Many people use these notebooks as diaries, to record goals and accomplishments, as well as for recording their appointments. Using one color to write work commitments and another for personal or family commitments, is a good idea. Coding tasks using a key such as "A," "B," "C" (A being most important, C as least important) can be helpful, but make sure you get feedback from you manager to prioritize your activities; what you think of as urgent may be of less importance to your manager. Once your have your obligations prioritized, schedule your time to tackle the most important items on your list before the less vital items.

"Retail professionals must be good time managers," says Stanley Guss, of the Retail Job Mart (on the Web at http://www.retailjobmart.com.) "They must be able to set priorities."

Here are Guss' rules for retail time management:

+ What affects the cash register today gets done first.
+ What affects the cash register tomorrow gets done second.
+ What affects the cash register next week gets done third.

MENTORS

A mentor, or "resource person," is someone who can teach you things about your career in retailing that you couldn't learn at school or by reading a book.

A mentor can be someone with whom you establish a long-term relationship that may last many years. Or, a mentor can be someone who takes you under his or her wing for a short time, such as a more experienced employee who helps to orient you the first days of your employment.

Finding a Mentor

Just as in the job search process, you'll have to be proactive in finding out who might be an effective, and willing, mentor to help you become the best retail professional you can be, and help you reach your career goals.

You may have identified people who will make a good mentor for you from your networking experiences. Although you should recruit people to mentor you from within your company, external mentors can be extremely valuable as well. Your boss can be a good resource to give you recommendations, and may introduce you to people who will be good mentors. People who volunteer information or advice to you are also potential mentors. In addition, from your daily life and in the workplace you'll observe people who model the kinds of skills you'd like to develop, who have the kind of reputation you'd like to acquire yourself, and who have qualities people admire. Don't be shy, ask these people to guide and train you!

Types of Mentors

There are two types of mentors. Although some people can be both, don't expect it. Different people display different strengths. One person with outstanding skills in merchandising, for example, may have less than exemplary management skills. If you want to learn both, don't look to that individual to teach you both.

One type of mentor—let's call her a *champion*—can provide guidance about ways to be successful in your company or in retailing (and business) in general. She can sponsor you for experiences that can advance your career, increase your visibility in the company, and introduce you to influential persons who can help you advance in your career. With any luck, this mentor is your supervisor or your manager's manager, but that isn't necessary—or even desirable—in every case.

From this type of mentor you can learn:

+ communication skills
+ industry trends
+ tips on getting along in business or in the company culture
+ career planning

Another type of mentor is more of a technical resource person. This person has more technical knowledge than you have, and is able and willing to share it with you. From this mentor you can learn:

+ retail problem-solving skills
+ customer service and retail sales skills
+ product knowledge
+ retailing or company-specific tricks and shortcuts

Nadine Smithline, Manager of Training and Communications at Federated Merchandise Group, advises all new retail professionals to "find a mentor once you're in the environment. Find someone at a higher level, who's been in retail—and with the company—for a while. Select someone you can talk with confidentially, who can show you the path. One of my mentors was someone I interviewed with; another was the senior vice president in the department I was working in. I reached out to each of them, told them I'd like the chance to have lunch with them. The relationships took off from there."

PROMOTING YOURSELF

People who don't promote themselves in the workplace will find themselves overshadowed by more visible colleagues.

To "promote" yourself doesn't mean giving yourself a raise or assigning yourself a better, flashier job title. It doesn't mean "grandstanding" by calling attention to how competitive or creative you are, while casting your coworkers in a bad light by comparison.

Promoting yourself does mean positioning yourself to be worthy of being promoted to a more responsible, higher-paying position by management. It means setting and achieving goals to learn new skills and knowledge and accepting opportunities to develop yourself and carry out additional responsibilities. It means demonstrating to your management that you have dedicated yourself to your current job. It means that you have met and exceeded all expectations in your present position. It means that you have been cooperative and flexible, and that you have shown initiative, creativity, and ethics in problem-solving and serving your customer.

"Volunteer!" encourages retailing expert Tom Russell. "Be open to special requests from the boss. Without a doubt, desire and willingness to go beyond what's expected are the single greatest factors used in promotions. Bosses value team-oriented people who are willing to do whatever it takes to get a job done. If a project needs someone to come in early or stay late, be the first to volunteer. You'll be surprised how often this approach pays off."

Promotions in retailing can come remarkably fast, especially in comparison with other industries. Promotability is linked to performance in retailing.

"I guarantee that in retailing today, most young people are moving or being promoted about every 9 to 12 months," notes Tom Russell.

A NOTE ABOUT EFFECTIVE SELLING

Retailing is about selling something—a product or a service—to someone who needs or wants it. It's also about getting someone to buy what you have, and persuading them that buying it is in their best interest as well as yours.

To be effective in this industry, plan on honing your salesmanship skills. You'll need them whether you launch your career talking to the public on the sales floor, or whether you're persuading a supplier or a colleague or manager at the corporate headquarters to do something you want them to.

Selling is not about dealing in any unethical or underhanded way. Selling someone a bad product won't make your customer happy, and your customer won't want to deal with you again. And *that* means they are likely to tell their friends and colleagues to avoid you as well.

To be an effective salesperson, therefore, you have to really understand your customer's needs, and you have to honestly try to satisfy their needs to the best of your ability.

Bob Langdon of Syracuse, New York, publishes the *Retailer News* on the World Wide Web at http://www.retailernews.com. In "Salespeople: Ask and You Shall Receive," Langdon says:

> Salespeople have a reputation for talking a lot. But many of the best
> salespeople don't talk much at all—they listen their way to success.

They don't try to talk people into buying; they ask questions and let their customers sell themselves.

Good questions accomplish many things: they provide you with information you need to move the sale forward, and they cause your prospects to think. Questions can help build rapport. They can instill confidence, present benefits, and overcome objections.

When prospects first walk into your store, ask them a question. Ask why they came to you. Are they shopping for themselves? For a gift? Have they been to any other stores?

Ask questions that build rapport and put prospects at ease. "Is that a handmade sweater? That's a beautiful car. How do you like it? What a cute little girl! What's her name?"

Ask questions that uncover needs. "Do you already own one? Why do you want a new one? What do you like best about your old cabinets? If you could build the perfect bathroom, what features would you build into it?"

Ask questions that help prospects feel their pain and yearn for your solution. "How often does that happen? What problems does that cause? How does that make you feel? How bad is it? What would happen if you did nothing?"

After presenting your solution to their problems, ask questions to gauge how you're doing. "Is that feature something you would use? How would that help make your life easier?"

Ask questions that uncover and overcome objections. "How do you feel about the style? Is that within your price range? How do you feel about the color? Is there anything that would prevent you from taking this home with you today?"

Finally, ask questions to close the sale. "Will that be cash or charge? Which would be better, delivery on Friday or Monday? You want fries with that?"

Remember, God gave us each two ears and one mouth. Use them in that proportion. Learn to ask the right questions at the right time to make selling easier and more enjoyable—for you and for your customers.

[Quoted by permission of Bob Langdon.]

QUALITY CUSTOMER SERVICE

If you're planning to make a successful career in retailing—and you are, because you've read this far!—you've got to endeavor in everything you do to exceed your customer's expectations. Here are some quality service tips for everyone who will spend some time as a sales associate, or in any capacity dealing with the public.

Anne M. Obarski owns Merchandise Concepts, a retail consulting firm in Pittsburgh, Pennsylvania. She helps retailers analyze and solve problems that cause their businesses to suffer. In "Five Secrets from a Secret Shopper" from the *Retailer News,* she says, "my 'retail snoops' business takes me all across the country, and everywhere I go I find the same shortcomings that stores need to focus on. It's unfortunate because the complaints that customers have are so easy to fix, if store management is willing to try." According to Obarski, the five most common infractions and their cures are:

1. **Always try to greet the customer warmly.** 95% of shoppers are never greeted upon entering a store. Worse yet, most are rarely approached while they are in the store.
2. **Display sincere interest in helping the customer.** 72% of shoppers complain that associates would not make eye contact when speaking with a customer and appeared to be "bothered" when the customer asked a question of the associate.
3. **Maintain a pleasant shopping atmosphere.** Shoppers can be the first to tell you if your racks are too tight or if your signage is clear and helpful. Dirty dressing rooms and untidy wrap desks can make the customer not want to come back to your store.
4. **Motivate store employees to always be productive.** "The sales associates were talking behind the wrap desk." "I didn't want to bother the sales girl because she was sitting behind the desk finishing her dinner." "The sales people were very busy folding merchandise, so I didn't ask for help." These are common complaints I hear all of the time. Associates need to be

productive but they also need to be aware that the customer is not an interruption of their work.

5. **Thank the customer for shopping in your store and ask them to return—even if they didn't buy!** Customers leave businesses every day feeling like they were just taken care of by a robot. 'Thanks, and have a nice day.' Did the associate really mean that, or was it just a way to keep the line moving? Remember, the last place that the customer usually remembers in a store is the wrap desk or checkout counter. If you want to increase repeat and referral business, make the last words you have with the customer ones that will make them happy they shopped in your store. So happy that they'll be back . . . and they'll bring their friends!

[Quoted by permission of Anne M. Obarski.]

ACHIEVE SUCCESS

People who succeed in retailing have a passion for it. They are committed to outdistancing their competition, to giving 110% to their employers and to their careers. Seeing their companies beat their competition by giving their customers better products, topping last years' sales figures, seeing their sales staff reach and exceed sales goals, gives them a feeling of intense satisfaction.

If you have a passion for retailing, do your best to show it. Go to work every day committed to giving your best to your employer, your coworkers and your customer. Prove to your employer that you value and appreciate the chance to succeed and contribute to the company's success. Develop positive and friendly relationships at work. Take classes to enhance your skills and knowledge. Find motivated mentors who will aid and support you and your efforts. Show everyone your best, and you will succeed in one of the most dynamic industries in the world today!

THE INSIDE TRACK

Who:	Nadine Smithline
What::	Manager of Training and Communication, Federated Merchandise Group
Where:	New York, NY
Education:	Bachelor's degree

Insider's Advice

Go out there and do an internship during college, or get as much retailing experience as possible. In addition, at whatever company you're with as an intern or employee, spend a day in the buying office or the corporate headquarters, to see what the environment is like. It's different than at a store. The environment is very fast-paced and demanding. Many jobs require an analytical mind, they're not as glamorous as some people think.

I completed a retail internship in college and was attracted to all the different areas: buying, human resources. I like it that you can change careers within one company.

Insider's Take on the Future

We are recruiting top-notch students. It's a challenging job market right now; we actively recruit on college campuses.

Companies want good candidates. We're looking for past leadership experience; we want confidence that they will be able to lead groups of people. We look to see what students have done to show they can analyze numbers; buying and planning, for example, are very analytical. We want candidates who are enthusiastic and creative. It's best if they have had some retailing experience.

APPENDIX A

PROFESSIONAL ASSOCIATIONS

This appendix includes a list of retailing-related trade and professional associations. Look into the ones that interest you while you are in training; they can provide lots of information about the particular retail niche they serve—information that can help you find the niche that's right for you. By joining the appropriate associations, you become eligible for the benefits and services each has to offer. Many organizations post employment opportunities, conduct training, and offer student memberships at a reduced rate.

RETAIL TRADE ORGANIZATIONS

American Craft Council
72 Spring St.
New York, NY 10012
212-274-0630
E-mail: acic@tmn.com

American Luggage Dealers Cooperative
610 Anacapa St.
Suite G
Santa Barbara, CA 93101
805-966-6909
Fax: 805-965-8566
E-mail: mialda@aol.com

American Truck Stop Owners Association
P.O. Box 4949
Winston-Salem, NC 27115-4949
910-744-5555
Fax: 910-744-1184

American Booksellers Association
828 S. Broadway
Tarrytown, NY 10591-5112
914-591-2665 / 800-637-0037
Fax: 914-591-2720
http://www.bookweb.org/
E-mail: info@bookweb.org

American Marketing Association
250 S. Wacker Dr.
Suite 200
Chicago, IL 60606
312-648-0536 / 800-262-1150
Fax: 312-993-7542
http://ama.org/
E-mail: info@ama.org

American Society of Transportation and Logistics
320 E. Water St.
Lock Haven, PA 17745-1490
717-748-8515
Fax: 717-748-9118
http://www.astl.org
E-mail: info@astl.org

Association for Retail Technology Standards
P.O. Box 15066
Reading, PA 19612-5055
Fax: 610-929-7336

Association of Store Design and Visual Merchandising Representatives
307 Cove Creek Ln.
Houston, TX 77042-1023
713-782-5533
Fax: 713-785-1114

Christian Booksellers Association
P.O. Box 200
Colorado Springs, CO 80901
719-576-7880 / 800-252-1950
Fax: 719-576-0798

Direct Marketing Association
1120 Ave. of the Americas
New York, NY 10036
212-768-7277
Fax: 212-391-1532
http://www.the-dma.org
E-mail: membership@the-dma.org

Food Marketing Institute
800 Connecticut Ave. NW
Suite 500
Washington, DC 20006-2701
202-452-8444
http://www.fmi.org/
E-mail: fmi@fmi.org

Footwear Distributors & Retailers of America
1319 F St. N.W.
Washington, DC 20004
202-737-5660
Fax: 202-638-2615
http://www.fdra.org
E-mail: fdra2@aol.com

Home Center Institute
5822 W. 74th St.
Indianapolis, IN 46278
317-299-0339
http://www.nrha.org/hci.html

Institute of Store Planners
25 N. Broadway
Tarrytown, NY 10591
914-332-1806 / 800-379-9912
Fax: 914-332-1541
http://www.ispo.org
E-mail: adminisp@ispo.org

International Association of Airport Duty Free Stores
1200 19th St. NW
Suite 300
Washington, DC 20036-2422
202-857-1184
Fax: 202-429-5154
http://www.iaadfs.org/
E-mail: iaadfs@sba.com

International Council of Shopping Centers
665 Fifth Ave.
New York, NY 10022
212-421-8181
Fax: 212-486-0849
http://www.ics.org

International Mass Retail Association
1901 Pennsylvania Ave. NW
10th Floor
Washington, DC 20006
202-861-0774
http://www.imra.org/
E-mail: Webmaster@ics.org

Jewelers of America
1185 6th Ave.
30th Floor
New York, NY 10036
212-768-8777 / 800-223-0673
Fax: 212-768-8087
http://www.jewelers.org/home.html

Museum Store Association
4100 E. Missisippi Ave. No. 800
Denver, CO 80246-3048
303-504-9223
Fax: 303-504-9585
http://www.canpo.org/orgs/711.htm

National Advisory Group, Convenience Stores/Petroleum Marketers Association
2063 Oak St.
Jacksonville, FL 32204-4492
904-384-1010
Fax: 904-387-3362
http://www.nag-net.com/
E-mail: info@nag-net.com

National Association of Beverage Retailers
101 River Rd.
Suite 108
Alexandria, VA 22314
703-683-4300
Fax: 703-683-8965

National Association of Casual Furniture Retailers
35 E. Wacker Dr.
Suite 500
Chicago, IL 60601-2105
312-782-5252 / 800-956-2237
Fax: 312-236-1140

National Association of Catalog Showroom Merchandisers
P.O. Box 736
East Northport, NY 11731
516-754-6041 / 800-334-4711
Fax: 516-754-7364

National Association of Chain Drug Stores
413 N. Lee St.
P.O. Box 1417-D49
Alexandria, VA 22313-1417
703-549-3001
Fax: 703-836-4869
http://www.nacds.org/
E-mail: homepage_info@nacds.org

National Association of College Stores
500 E. Lorain St.
Oberlin, OH 44074
216-775-7777 / 800-622-7498
Fax: 216-775-4769
http://www.nacs.org

National Association of Convenience Stores
1605 King St.
Alexandria, VA 22314-2792
703-684-3600
Fax: 703-836-4564
http://www.cstorecentral.com/public/nacs/052.htm
E-mail: nacs@cstorecentral.com

National Association of Men's Sportswear Buyers
500 5th Ave.
Suite 1425
New York, NY 10110
212-391-8580
Fax: 212-827-0166

National Association of Purchasing Management
2055 E. Centennial Circle
P.O. Box 22160
Tempe, AZ 85285-2160
602-752-6276 / 800-888-6276
Fax: 602-752-7890
http://www.napm.org/
E-mail: custsvc@napm.org

National Association of Resale and Thrift Shops
P.O. Box 80707
St. Clair Shores, MI 48080-0707
810-294-6700 / 800-544-0751
Fax: 810-294-6776
http://www.iaadfs.org/
E-mail: Webmaster@NARTS.org
E-mail: MissAdele@aol.com

National Association of Retail Dealers of America/North American Retailers of America
10 E. 22nd St.
Suite 310
Lombard, IL 60148
630-953-8950 / 800-621-0298
Fax: 630-953-8957
http://www.NARDA.com
E-mail:nardahdq@aol.com

National Association of Retail Merchandising Services
P.O. Box 906
Plover, WI 54467-0906
715-342-0948 / 888-526-2767
Fax: 715-342-1943
http://www.narms.com
E-mail: info@narms.com

National Grocers Association
1825 Samuel Morse Dr.
Reston, VA 20910
703-437-5300
Fax: 703-437-7768

National Home Furnishings Association
P.O. Box 2396
High Point, NC 27261
910-883-1650 / 800-888-9590 ext. 335
Fax: 910-883-1195
http://www.homefurnish.com/NHFA/home.htm
E-mail: nhfaa@homefurnish.com

National Lumber and Building Material Dealers Association
666 Pennsylvania Ave. SE
Washington, DC 20003-4006
202-547-2230
Fax: 202-547-7640
http://www.nlmda.org/
E-mail: nlbmda@nlbmda.org

National Nutritional Foods Association
3931 MacArthur Blvd.
No. 101
Newport Beach, CA 92660-3021
714-622-6272 / 800-966-6632
Fax: 714-622-6266
http://www.nnfa.org/
E-mail: Webmaster@NNFA.org
E-mail: nnfa@aol.com

National Retail Federation
325 7th St. NW
Suite 1000
Washington, DC 20004-2802
202-783-7971 / 800-673-4692
Fax: 202-737-2849
http://www.nrf.com
E-mail: Webmaster@nrf.com

National Retail Hardware Association
5822 W. 74th St.
Indianapolis, IN 46278
317-290-0338 / 800-722-4424
Fax: 317-328-4354
http://www.nrha.org
E-mail: Nrha@lquest.net

National Shoe Retailers Association
9861 Broken Land Pkwy. Suite 255
Columbia, MD 21046-1151
410-381-8282 / 800-673-8446
Fax: 410-381-1167
http://nsra.org
E-mail: Mbrinfo@nsra.org

National Sporting Goods Association
Lake Center Plaza Building
1699 Wall St.
Mt. Prospect, IL 60056-5780
847-439-4000
Fax: 847-439-0111
http://www.nsga.org/main.html
E-mail: HYPERLINK mailto:Nsgal1699@aol.com

APPENDIX B

ADDITIONAL RESOURCES

After you've read this book and have a good idea of what steps you need to take to accomplish your goals, review the items in this Appendix for books and magazines to look at and places to go for information about accredited schools. These items will provide more specific information and advice on areas you need help in.

BOOKS

Career Change

Helfland, David P. CareerChange: *Everything You Need to Know to Meet Challenges and Take Control of Your Career*. Lincolnwood, IL: VGM Career Horizons. 1995.

Kanchier, Carole. *Dare to Change Your Job and Your Life*. 2nd ed. Indianapolis: JIST Works. 1995.

Colleges

Peterson's Guide to Four-Year Colleges. Princeton, NJ: Peterson's. Annual.

Peterson's Guide to Two-Year Colleges. Princeton, NJ: Peterson's. Annual.

The Princeton Review. *The Complete Book of Colleges 1998.* New York: Random House, The Princeton Review. 1997.

Cover Letters

Beatty, Richard H. *The Perfect Cover Letter.* 2nd ed. New York: John Wiley & Sons. 1997.

Besson, Taunee. *The Wall Street Journal National Business Employment Weekly: Cover Letters.* 2nd ed. New York: John Wiley & Sons. 1996.

Marler, Patty and Jan Bailey Mattia. *Cover Letters Made Easy.* Lincolnwood, IL: VGM Career Horizons. 1996.

Dress, Appearance, and Etiquette

Fox, Grace. *Office Etiquette and Protocol: The Basics Made Easy.* New York: LearningExpress. 1998.

Molloy, John T. *The New John Molloy's New Dress for Success.* New York: Warner Books. 1997.

Sutterfield, Mark. *VGM's Complete Guide to Career Etiquette: From Job Search through Career Advancement.* Lincolnwood, IL: VGM Career Horizons. 1995.

Financial Aid/Scholarships

College Costs & Financial Aid Handbook. 18th ed. New York: College Entrance Examination Board. 1998.

Davis, Kristen. *Financing College: How to Use Savings, Financial Aid, Scholarships, and Loans to Afford the School of Your Choice.* Washington, DC: Random House/Kiplinger. 1996.

Kirby, Debra M. *Fund Your Way Through College.* Detroit: Visible Ink Press. 1993.

Peterson's College Money Handbook 1998. 15th ed. Princeton, NJ: Peterson's. 1997.

Schlachter, Gail Ann and R. David Weber. *College Student's Guide To Merit and Other No-Need Funding.* San Carlos, CA: Reference Service Press. 1995.

Schlachter, Gail Ann and R. David Weber. *High School Senior's Guide To Merit and Other No-Need Funding.* San Carlos, CA: Reference Service Press. 1995.

Scholarships, Fellowships, and Loans. Boston: Gale Research. 1993.

Internet Job Hunting

Bolles, Richard N. *Job Hunting on the Internet.* Berkeley, CA: Ten Speed Press. 1997.

Riley, Margaret, Frances Roehm and Steve Oserman. *The Guide to Internet Job Searching.* Lincolnwood, IL: NTC Publishing Group with the Public Library Association. 1998.

Internships

The Princeton Review. *The Internship Bible.* 1998 ed. New York: Random House. 1997.

Interviewing

Fein, Richard. *111 Dynamite Ways to Ace Your Job Interview.* Manassas Park, VA: Impact. 1996.

Fry, Ron. *101 Great Answers to the Toughest Interview Questions.* 3rd ed. Franklin Lakes, NJ: Book-Mart Press. 1996.

Hellman, Paul. *Ready, Aim, You're Hired!: How to Job-Interview Successfully Anytime, Anywhere with Anyone.* New York: AMACOM. 1986.

Kennedy, Joyce Lain. *Job Interviews for Dummies.* Foster City, CA: IDG Books. 1996.

Medley, H. Anthony. *Sweaty Palms: The Neglected Art of Being Interviewed.* Berkeley, CA: Ten Speed Press.1992.

Job Hunting and Career Planning Guidance

Bolles, Richard N. *What Color Is Your Parachute?* Berkeley, CA: Ten Speed Press. Updated annually.

Williams, Marcia P, and Sue A. Cubbage. *The 1997 National Job Hotline Directory.* New York: McGraw-Hill. 1997.

Figler, Howard E. *The Complete Job Search Handbook: Presenting the Skills You Need to Get Any Job, and Have A Good Time Doing It.* New York: Henry Holt. 1988.

Jackson, Tom. *Guerrilla Tactics in the New Job Market.* New York: Bantam Books. 1991.

Resnick, R. Linda and Kerry H. Pechter. *A Big Splash in a Small Pond: Finding a Great Job in a Small Business.* New York: Simon and Schuster. 1994.

Sonnenblick, Carol, Michaele Basciano, and Kim Crabbe. *Job Hunting Made Easy: 20 Simple Steps to Coming Up a Winner.* New York: LearningExpress. 1997.

Wegmann, Robert, Robert Chapman, and Miriam Johnson. *Work in the New Economy: Careers and Job Seeking into the 21st Century.* Indianapolis: JIST Works. 1989.

Miscellaneous

National Retail Security Survey. Gainseville, FL: University of Florida. Annual.

Wright, John. *The American Almanac of Jobs and Salaries.* New York: Avon Books. 1996.

Finerty, Gregory S., Robert M. Kauffman and Robert M. Zimmerman. *Retail Accounting and Financial Control.* 5th ed. New York: John Wiley & Sons, Inc. 1990.

Networking

Boe, Anne, and Bettie B. Youngs. *Is Your "Net" Working?: A Complete Guide to Building Contacts and Career Visibility.* New York: John Wiley & Sons. 1989.

Krannich, Ronald L. and Caryl Rae Krannich. *The New Network Your Way to Job and Career Success.* 3rd ed. Manassas, VA: Impact. 1993.

Shelly, Susan. *Networking for Novices: The Basics Made Easy.* New York: LearningExpress. 1998.

Stoodley, Martha. *Information Interviewing: How to Tap Your Hidden Job Market.* Garrett Park, MD: Garrett Park Press. 1996.

Resume Writing

Kennedy, Joyce Lain and TJ Morrow. *Electronic Resume Revolution.* New York: John Wiley & Sons. 1995.

Parker, Yana. *The Resume Catalog: 200 Damn Good Examples.* Berkeley, CA. Ten Speed Press. 1996.

Parker, Yana. *The Damn Good Resume Guide.* Berkeley, CA: Ten Speed Press. 1996.

Smith, Rebecca. *Electronic Resumes and Online Networking: How to Use the Internet to Do a Better Job Search, Including a Complete, Up-To-Date Resource Guide.* Hawthorne, NJ: The Career Press. 1999.

Rosenberg, Arthur D. and David V. Hizer. *The Resume Handbook: How to Write Outstanding Resumes and Cover Letters for Every Situation.* 3rd ed. Holbrook, MA: Adams Media Corporation. 1996.

Retail Careers

Beisel, John L. *Contemporary Retailing.* 2nd ed. New York: Macmillan College Division. 1993.

Koester, Pat. *Careers in Fashion Retailing.* New York: The Rosen Publishing Group. 1990.

Dolber, Roslyn. *Opportunities in Fashion Careers.* Lincolnwood, IL: VGM Career Horizons. 1992.

Hartley, Robert F. *Retailing: Challenge & Opportunity.* 3rd ed. New York: Houghton & Mifflin. 1984.

Jernigan, Marian H. and Cynthia R. Easterling. *Fashion Merchandising and Marketing.* New York: Macmillian. 1990.

Jones, Ken & Simmons, Jim. *The Retail Environment.* New York: Van Nostrand Reinhold. 1990.

Stone, Elaine. *Fashion Merchandising: An Introduction.* New York: Glencoe/Macmillan. 1989.

Retail Company Financial Information

Fairchild Financial Manual of Retail Stores. New York, NY: Fairchild Publications. Annual.

Retail Yearbook. Columbus, OH: Management Horizons, a division of Price Waterhouse. Annual. Two volumes.

The Retailing Industry. Chicago, IL: First National Bank of Chicago. Annual.

The Retail Monitor. Ontario, Canada: Coopers & Lybrand Consulting. Monthly.

Retailing Dictionaries

Calasibetta, Charlotte Mankey. *Fairchild's Dictionary of Fashion.* 2nd ed. New York: Fairchild Publications. 1988.

Ostrow, Rona and Sweetman R. Smith. *The Dictionary of Retailing.* New York: Fairchild Publications. 1984.

Rosenberg, Jerry. *Dictionary of Retailing and Merchandising.* New York: John Wiley & Sons. 1995.

Retailing Directories to Stores and Store Locations

The Book on Value Retailing. Clearwater, FL: Value Retail News.

CSG Market Directories. Tampa, FL: CSG Information Services.

Major Mass Market Merchandisers. New York Salesman's Guide. [This is one of several directories published by Salesman's Guide that gives information on retailers. There are also several directories of buyers for the retail industry. One such directory is titled *Buying Offices & Accounts;* it lists 219 Resident Buying Offices representing over 7,000 stores.]

The Off-Price Retail Directory. Clearwater, FL: Value Retail News.

Phelon, Kenneth W., ed. *Sheldon's Retail Directory.* Fairview, NJ: Phelon, Sheldon & Marsar.

Retail Management

Levy, Michael, and Barton Weitz. *Retailing Management.* 3rd ed. Burr Ridge, IL: Irwin/McGraw Hill, 1998.

Lewison, Dale J. *Retailing.* 5th ed. New York: MacMillan. 1994.

Diamond, Jay and Gerald Pintel. *Retail Buying.* New York: Prentice Hall. 1996.

Retail Shopping Center Directories

Chain Store Guide Directory. New York: Lebhar-Friedman Publications. Annual.

Directory of Major Malls. Spring Valley, NY: MJJTM Publications Corp. Annual.

Retail Tenant Directory. Clearwater, FL: Monitor, Inc. Annual.

Shopping Center Directory. Chicago, IL: National Research Bureau. Annual. Four volumes.

Standardized Test Preparation

Kaplan's ACT: Powerful Strategies to Help You Score Higher: 1998 edition. New York: Simon & Schuster. 1997

Katyman, John and Adam Robinson. *The Princeton Review's Cracking the SAT & PSAT: 1998 edition.* New York: Random House. 1997.

Student Success/Basic Skills

Chesla, Elizabeth. *Read Better, Remember More: The Basics Made Easy*. New York: LearningExpress. 1997.

Chesla, Elizabeth. *Improve Your Writing for Work: The Basics Made Easy*. New York: LearningExpress. 1997.

Ellis, David. *Becoming a Master Student*. 8th ed. New York: Houghton-Mifflin. 1997.

Robinovitz, Judith. *Practical Math Success in 20 Minutes a Day*. 2nd ed. New York: LearningExpress. 1998.

Studying

Coman, Marcia J. and Kathy L. Heavers. *How to Improve Your Study Skills*. 2nd ed. Lincolnwood, IL: NTC Publishing. 1998.

Fry, Ron. *Ron Fry's How to Study Program*. 4th ed. Hawthorne, NJ: Career Press. 1996.

Wood, Gail. *How to Study*. New York: LearningExpress. 1996.

MAGAZINES

Here are the names of several retailing magazines to help you investigate trends and see what part of this exciting industry might suit you best.

Trade Publications

Retail managers use the publications listed below to learn about industry trends and methods for improving the profitability of their business. Most college or public libraries do not have these trade publications. However, students can write or call the publisher and get information about the publication with some sample issues. In addition, many of these publications collect information about a specific aspect of the retail industry, which are printed in separate reports and made available on request.

Accessories
Business Journals, Inc.
P.O. Box 5550
Norwalk, CT 06814
203-853-6015

Advertising Age
Crain Communications, Inc.
740 Rush St.
Chicago, IL 60611-2590
800-678-9595

American Booksellers Association
Booksellers Publishing, Inc.
828 S. Broadway
Tarrytown, NY 10591-5112
800-637-0037
http://www.bookweb.org

American Retailer
American Retailer, Inc.
21 W. Delelah Rd.
Pleasantville, NJ 08232
609-646-2692

Apparel Merchandising
Lebhar-Friedman, Inc.
425 Park Ave.
New York, NY 10022
212-756-5269
http://www.lf.com

Auto Merchandising News
Mortimer Communication, Inc.
P.O. Box 1185
Fairfield, CT 06430
203-384-9323

Billboard
Billboard Communication, Inc.
1515 Broadway, 39th fl.
New York, NY 10036
212-764-7300
http://www.billboard.com

Body Fashions/Intimate Apparel 34A
Advanstar Communications, Inc.
7500 Old Oak Blvd.
Cleveland, OH 44130
216-826-2839
http://www.bfia.com

Business of Fur
Fur Publishing Plus, Inc.
19 West 21st St.
New York, NY 10001
212-727-1210

California Apparel News
MNM Publishing Corp.
110 E. 9th St. A777
Los Angeles, CA 90079-1929
213-627-3737
http://www.apparelnews.com

Chain Store Age
Lebhar-Friedman
425 Park Ave.
New York, NY 10022
212-756-5000

Chicago Apparel News
MNM Publishing Corp.
The Apparel Center
350 N. Orleans, Suite 52-107
Chicago, IL 60654
312-670-2230

Children's Business
Fairchild Publications
7 W. 34th St.
New York, NY 10001
212-630-4199
http://www.fairchildpub.com/home.htm

College Store Executive
Executive Business Media
P.O. Box 1500, 825 Old Country Road
Westbury, NY 11590
516-334-3030

Consumer Electronics 122
Fairchild Publications
7 W. 34th St.
New York, NY 10001
212-630-4199

Convenience Store Management
Capital Cities
825 Seventh Ave., 6th fl.
New York, NY 10019

Convenience Store News
MacFadden Trade Publications
233 Park Ave. S. 6th fl.
New York, NY 10003
212-780-2300
http://www.csnews.com/index.html

Daily News Record
Fairchild Publications
7 W. 34th St.
New York, NY 10001
212-630-3600
http://www.dailynewsrecord.com

Dallas Apparel News
MNM Publishing Corp.
2300 Stemmons Freeway, M5F15
Apparel Mart
Dallas, TX 675258
214-631-6089

Decorating Retailer
National Decorating Products
Association
1050 N. Lindbergh Blvd.
St. Louis, MO 63132
314-991-3470

Direct Marketing
Hoke Communications, Inc.
224 Seventh St.
Garden City, NY 11530
516-746-6700 / 800-229-6700
http://www.directmarket.co.uk

Discount Merchandiser
Schwartz Publications
233 Park Ave. South, 10th fl.
New York, NY 10003
212-979-4860

Discount Store News
Lebhar-Friedman, Inc.
425 Park Ave.
New York, NY 10022
212-756-5000
http://www.DiscountStoreNews.com/

Display & Design Ideas
Shore Communications, Inc.
6255 Barfield Road, Suite 200
Atlanta, GA 30328-4300
800-241-9034

Do-It-Yourself Retailing
National Retail Hardware Association
5822 W. 74th St.
Indianapolis, IN 46278
317-297-1190
http://www.nrha.org

DM News: The Newspaper of Direct Marketing
Mill Hollow Corp.
19 West 21st St.
New York, NY 10010
212-741-2095

Earnshaw's Infants, Girls and Boys Wear Review
Earnshaw Publications, Inc.
225 West 34th St.
New York, NY 10001
212-563-2742

Fancy Foods
Talcott Communication, Inc.
20 N. Wacker Dr., Suite 3230
Chicago, IL 60606-3102
312-849-2220
http://talcott.com/fancyfood/fancyfood.htm

The Fashion Galleria
Darlene Griggs Enterprises
4100 McEwen, Suite 196
Dallas, TX 75244
214-386-5228

Fashion Jewelry Plus
Larkin-Pluznick-Larkin, Inc.
P.O. Box 9103, 100 Wells Ave.
Newton, MA 02159
617-964-5100

Footwear News 79
Fairchild Publications
7 W. 34th St.
New York, NY 10001
212-630-4199
http://footwearnews.com/horne.htm

Furniture Retailer
Pace Communications
1301 Carolina St.
Greensboro, NC 27401
919-378-6065
http://www.pacecomm.com

Furniture Today
Cahners Business Newspaper
Division of Reed Elsevier, Inc.
7025 Albert Pick Road
Greensboro, NC 27409
910-605-0121
http://www.cahners.com/default.htm

Gifts & Decorative Accessories
Geyer-McAlister Publications, Inc.
51 Madison Ave.
New York, NY 10010
212-689-4411

Gourmet News
United Publications, Inc.
Box 1056
Yarmouth, ME 04096
207-846-0600

The Gourmet Retailer
Sterling Southeast, Inc.
3301 Ponce De Leon Blvd., No. 300
Coral Gables, FL 33134
305-893-8771

Grocery Distribution
Grocery Market Publications
455 S. Frontage Rd., Suite 116
Burr Ridge, IL 60521
708-986-8767

Grocery Marketing
Delta Communications, Inc.
455 N. Cityfront Plaza Dr., 24th fl.
Chicago, IL 60611
312-222-2000

Hardware Age
Chilton Company, Inc.
Chilton Way
Radnor, PA 19089
215-964-4269

HFD (Home Furnishings Dealers)
HFN (Home Furnishings Network)
Fairchild Publications
7 W. 34th St.
New York, NY 10001
212-630-4000 / 800-247-2160

Home Improvement Centers
Vance Publishing Corp.
400 Knightsbridge Parkway
Lincolnshire, IL 60069
312-634-4379

Home Textiles Today
The Cahners Publishing Company
Division of Reed Publishing USA
275 Washington St.
Newton, MA 02158-1630
800-395-2329

Housewares
Advanstar Communications, Inc.
7500 Old Oak Blvd.
Cleveland, OH 44130

Inside Retailing
Lebhar-Friedman, Inc.
425 Park Ave.
New York, NY 10022.
212-756-5000

Leather Today
Fur Publishing Plus, Inc.
19 West 21st St., Suite 403
New York, NY 10001
212-727-1210

Magazine and Bookseller
North American Publishing Company
322 Eighth Ave., 3rd fl.
New York, NY 10001
212-620-7330
E-mail: editor@mb.rapco.com

Marketing News
American Marketing Association
250 South Wacker Dr., Suite 200
Chicago, IL 60606-5819
312-648-0536

Mass Market Retailers
Racher Press, Inc.
220 Fifth Ave.
New York, NY 10001
212-213-6000

Modern Jeweler National
P.O. Box 1414
Lincolnshire, IL 60069-1414
708-634-2800/800-621-2845

Modern Grocer
Grocers Publishing Company
15 Emerald St.
Hackensack, NJ 07601
201-488-1800

Modern Tire Dealer
Bill Automotive Group
P.O. Box 3599, 341 White Pond Drive
Akron, OH 44309-3599
330-867-4401
E-mail: 753.0308@mcimail.
http://www.mtdealer.com

Monitor
Monitor's Insider Trade Dimensions
263 Tresser Blvd., 5th fl.
Stamford, CT 06901-3202
203-977-7636

National Home Center News
Lebhar-Friedman
425 Park Ave.
New York, NY 10022
212-756-5000

New York Apparel News
MNM Publishing Corp.
1501 Broadway, Suite 1508
New York, NY. 10018
212-221-8288

Non-Foods Merchandising
Cardinal Business Media, Inc.
200 Connecticut Ave., Suite 5-0
Norwalk, CT 06854
203-838-9100

Private Label Product News
252 W. Swamp Road, Suite 13
Doylestown, PA 18901
215-230-4400

Progressive Grocer
Progressive Grocer Associates
23 Old King's Highway South
Darien, CT 06820
203-655-1600
http://www.progressivegrocer.com

Retail Info Systems News (RIS News)
Edgell Enterprises, Inc.
10 W. Hanover Ave., Suite 107
Randolph, NJ 07869
201-895-3300

Retail Store Image
INTERTEC Publications
P.O. Box 41369
Nashville, TN 37204-1369
615-377-3322

RT: The Magazine of Retail Technology
Progressive Grocer Associates
23 Old King's Highway South
Darien, CT 06820
203-655-1600
Fax: 203-656-3800

Shopping Center World
Communications Channel Inc.
6151 Powers Ferry Rd. NW
Atlanta, GA 30339-2941
770-955-2500
http://www.intertec.com/pubs/scw.htm

Shopping Centers Today
International Council of Shopping
Centers
665 Fifth Ave.
New York, NY 10022
212-421-8181

Sporting Goods Dealer
PTN Publishing Corp.
455 Broad Nallow Road
Melville, NY 11747
516-846-2700

Sports Trend
Shore-Varrone, Inc.
6255 Barfield Rd. NE, Suite 200
Atlanta, GA 30328-4300
404-252-8831

Sportswear International
Opal Publishing
29 W. 38th St., 15th fl.
New York, NY 10018
212-768-8450

Stores
NRF Enterprises, Inc.
325 7th St. NW, Suite 1000
Washingon, DC 20004-2802
202-783-7971

Supermarket Business
Howfrey Communications
1086 Teaneck Rd.
Teaneck, NJ 07666-4838
201-833-1900

Supermarket News
Fairchild Publications
7 W. 34th St.
New York, NY 10001
212-630-4199

Toy and Hobby World
Toy & Hobby Retailer
Thomson Retail Press
345 Park Ave.
New York, NY 10010
212-686-7744

Value Retail News
Off-Price News
15950 Bay Vista Drive, Suite 250
Clearwater, FL 34620-3131
813-536-4047

VM + SD (Visual Merchandising and
Store Design)
ST Publications
407 Gilbert Ave.
Cincinnati, OH 45202
513-421-2050

Women's Wear Daily
Fairchild Publications
7 W. 34th St.
New York, NY 10001
212-630-4199

Young Fashions Magazine
WFC, Inc.
119 Fifth Ave.
New York, NY 10003
212-677-7040

COLLEGE ACCREDITING AGENCIES

Here's a list of national and regional accrediting associations you can contact to see if your preferred school is accredited. You can also request that the agency send you a list of schools it accredits.

American Assembly of Collegiate Schools of Business
600 Emerson Road, Suite 300
St. Louis, Missouri 63141-6762
314-872-8481

Accrediting Commission of Career Schools and Colleges of Technology
2101 Wilson Boulevard, Suite 302
Arlington, VA 22201
703- 247-4212
Fax: 703-247-4533
http://www.accsct.org/
E-mail: info@accsct.org

Accrediting Council for Independent Colleges and Schools
750 First St., Suite 980
Washington, DC 20002-4242
202-336-6780
Fax: 220-842-2593
http://www.acics.org
E-mail: info@acics.org

American Association of Family and Consumer Sciences
Council for Accreditation
1555 King St.
Alexandria, VA 22314
703-706-4600
Fax: 703-706-4663
http://www.aafcs.org/
E-mail: info@aafcs.org

Association Of Collegiate Business Schools and Programs
7007 College Blvd., No. 420
Overland Park, KS 66211-1524
913-339-9356
Fax: 913-339-6626
E-mail: acbsp@aol.com

Council For Higher Education Accreditation
One Dupont Circle NW, Suite 510
Washington DC, 20036-1135
202-955-6126
Fax: 202-955-6129
http://www.chea.org/directories/regional.htm
E-mail: chea@chea.org

Middle States Association of Colleges and Schools
3624 Market St.
Philadelphia, PA 19104-2680
215-662-5606
Fax: 215-662-5501
http://www.css-msa.org/
E-mail: info@msache.org

New England States Association of Schools and Colleges
209 Burlington Dr.
Bedford, MA 01730-1433
617-271-0022
Fax: 617-271-0950
http://www.neasc.org/
E-mail: info@neasc.org

North Central Association of Colleges and Schools
159 N. Dearborn St.
Chicago, IL 60601
Toll Free: 800-621-7440
312-263-0456

Fax: 312-263-7462

http://www.ncacihe.org/

E-mail: info@ncacihe.org

Northwest Association of Schools and Colleges

Boise State University

1901 University Dr.

Boise, ID 83725

208-334-3226

Fax: 208-334-3228

E-mail: selman@u.washington.edu

Southern Association of Colleges and Schools

1866 Southern Ln.

Decatur, GA 30033-4097

404-679-4500

Fax: 404-679-4558

http://www.sacs.org/

E-mail: Dkrone@sacscoc.org

Western Association of Schools and Colleges/ Accrediting Commission for Community and Junior Colleges

3402 Mendocino Ave.

Santa Rosa, Ca 95403-2244

707-375-7711

Fax: 707-569-9179

E-mail: ACCJC@aol.com

Accrediting Agency Responsible for Each State

State	Regional Accrediting Agency	State	Regional Accrediting Agency
Alabama	SACS	Nebraska	NCACS
Alaska	NASs	Nevada	NASC
American Samoa	WASC	New Hampshire	NEASC
Arizona	NCACS	New Jersey	MSACS
Arkansas	NCACS	New Mexico	NCACS
California	WASC	New York	MSACS
Colorado	NCACS	North Carolina	SACS
Connecticut	NEASC	North Dakota	NCACS
Delaware	MSACS	Northern Marianas	WASC
District of Columbia	MSACS	Ohio	NCACS
Florida	SACS	Oklahoma	NCACS
Georgia	SACS	Oregon	NASC
Guam	WASC	Pacific Islands	WASC
Hawaii	WASC	Pennsylvania	MSACS
Idaho	NASC	Puerto Rico	MSACS
Illinois	NCACS	Republic of Panama	MSACS
Indiana	NCACS	Rhode Island	NEASC
Iowa	NCACS	South Dakota	NCACS
Kansas	NCACS	Tennessee	SACS
Kentucky	SACS	Texas	SACS
Louisiana	SACS	U.S. Virgin Islands	MSACS
Maine	NEASC	Utah	NASC
Maryland	MSACS	Vermont	NEASC
Massachusetts	NEASC	Virginia	SACS
Michigan	NCACS	Washington	NASC
Minnesota	NCACS	West Virginia	NCACS
Mississippi	SACS	Wisconsin	NCACS
Missouri	NCACS	Wyoming	NCACS
Montana	NASC		

APPENDIX C

RETAILING SKILL STANDARDS

Do you want to set goals for training, education, and performance in retailing? Review the standards in this appendix to prepare yourself to become the exceptional retail professional you want to be.

The National Retail Federation (NRF) has produced a set of retail-specific job skill standards for the Professional Sales Associate. These standards were developed with input from retail executives, managers and sales associates all over the country. They describe what workers in the retail industry need to learn, and what employers should expect when they are looking to hire, train, and promote employees.

Reviewing the NRF Retail Skill Standards can help you:

- evaluate your potential for success in a retail career
- assess your retail knowledge and skills
- keep a record of your job performance, which can help you design a "stand-out" resume

- develop retailing skills that you can take with you from job to job as your career progresses
- identify areas in which you need further education and training
- excel as a productive, "promotable" member of a retail team and company

Professional Sales Associate Key Duties and Tasks

There are six groups, or modules, of duties. These are the "building blocks" essential for high performance as a Professional Sales Associate. With the permission of the NRF and the National Retail Institute (the education and training arm of the NRF), here are the modules, key tasks, and some of the specific elements required for each key task.

Module 1: Provide Personalized Customer Service

Key Task: Initiate customer contact

- determine customer's needs by listening and asking questions
- give customer appropriate greeting
- refer customer to another department/store

Key Task: Build customer relations
- follow through on commitments made to customer
- handle customer complaints
- balance responsive phone service with in-store service

Module 2: Sell and Promote Products

Key Task: Determine customer needs

- listen and ask open-ended questions
- acquire and apply product knowledge
- verify product that is appropriate for customer use

Key Task: Build the sale

- motivate customer to return for future purchases
- sell customer additional or related merchandise
- handle customer returns; transform into new sale

Key Task: Close the sale

- assist customer in making purchase decision

  ◆ handle transactions and related paperwork
  ◆ open, maintain, and close cash register

Module 3: Monitor Inventory
Key Task: Take inventory

  ◆ check in merchandise against paperwork
  ◆ assure accurate pricing on merchandise
  ◆ locate merchandise through inventory system

Key Task: Transfer inventory

  ◆ prepare returned merchandise for resale
  ◆ initiate and/or respond to requests for merchandise transfer
  ◆ identify damaged items and handle appropriately

Module 4: Maintain Appearance of Department/Store
Key Task: Maintain stock, customer service, and selling areas

  ◆ organize and maintain supplies
  ◆ clean customer service and selling areas
  ◆ report need for repairs or replacement

Key Task: Maintain product presentation and displays

  ◆ arrange merchandise
  ◆ relay feedback from customers on the effectiveness of displays
  ◆ maintain displays following company's display guidelines

Module 5: Protect Company Assets
Key Task: Identify and prevent loss

  ◆ alert customer to your presence/availability
  ◆ account for items after customer use of dressing rooms
  ◆ report stock shrinkage

Key Task: Follow safety procedures

  ◆ report safety problems in the department/store
  ◆ follow emergency procedures
  ◆ maintain accurate records

Module 6: Work as Part of a Department/Store Team

Key Task: Support co-workers

- share ideas and information about selling, marketing, products, customers, feedback, and loss control
- assist/turnover sale to co-worker to better serve customer and company
- assist with training and orientation of new employees

Key Task: Create customer advantage

- research the competition (products, prices, and services)
- provide manager and peers with feedback on competition
- develop personal and professional goals

For more information about, or a copy of, the Professional Sales Associate skill standards, contact the National Retail Institute at 325 7th Street NW, Suite 1000, Washington, DC 20004. You can also call them at 1-800-673-4692. Or, check out the NRF Web site at http://www.nrf.org and follow the links.

Order Form

CALIFORNIA EXAMS

___ @ $35.00   CA Allied Health
___ @ $35.00   CA Corrections Officer
___ @ $35.00   CA Firefighter
___ @ $20.00   CA Law Enforcement Career Guide
___ @ $35.00   CA Police Officer
___ @ $30.00   CA Postal Worker
___ @ $35.00   CA State Police
___ @ $17.95   CBEST (California Basic Educational
               Skills Test)

NEW JERSEY EXAMS

___ @ $35.00   NJ Allied Health
___ @ $35.00   NJ Corrections Officer
___ @ $35.00   NJ Firefighter
___ @ $20.00   NJ Law Enforcement Career Guide
___ @ $35.00   NJ Police Officer
___ @ $30.00   NJ Postal Worker
___ @ $35.00   NJ State Police

TEXAS EXAMS

___ @ $17.95   TASP (Texas Academic Skills Program)
___ @ $32.50   TX Allied Health
___ @ $35.00   TX Corrections Officer
___ @ $35.00   TX Firefighter
___ @ $20.00   TX Law Enforcement Career Guide
___ @ $35.00   TX Police Officer
___ @ $30.00   TX Postal Worker
___ @ $29.95   TX Real Estate Exam
___ @ $30.00   TX State Police

NEW YORK EXAMS

___ @ $30.00   New York City Firefighter
___ @ $25.00   NYC Police Officer
___ @ $35.00   NY Allied Health
___ @ $35.00   NY Corrections Officer
___ @ $35.00   NY Firefighter
___ @ $20.00   NY Law Enforcement Career Guide
___ @ $30.00   NY Postal Worker
___ @ $35.00   NY State Police
___ @ $30.00   Suffolk County Police Officer

MASSACHUSETTS EXAMS

___ @ $30.00   MA Allied Health
___ @ $30.00   MA Police Officer
___ @ $30.00   MA State Police Exam

ILLINOIS EXAMS

___ @ $25.00   Chicago Police Officer
___ @ $25.00   Illinois Allied Health

FLORIDA EXAMS

___ @ $32.50   FL Allied Health
___ @ $35.00   FL Corrections Officer
___ @ $20.00   FL Law Enforcement Career Guide
___ @ $35.00   FL Police Officer
___ @ $30.00   FL Postal Worker

REGIONAL EXAMS

___ @ $29.95   AMP Real Estate Sales Exam
___ @ $29.95   ASI Real Estate Sales Exam
___ @ $30.00   Midwest Police Officer Exam
___ @ $30.00   Midwest Firefighter Exam
___ @ $17.95   PPST (Praxis I)
___ @ $29.95   PSI Real Estate Sales Exam
___ @ $25.00   The South Police Officer Exam
___ @ $25.00   The South Firefighter Exam

NATIONAL EDITIONS

___ @ $20.00   Allied Health Entrance Exams
___ @ $14.95   ASVAB (Armed Services Vocational Aptitu
               Battery): Complete Preparation Guide
___ @ $12.95   ASVAB Core Review
___ @ $17.95   Border Patrol Exam
___ @ $12.95   Bus Operator Exam
___ @ $15.00   Federal Clerical Exam
___ @ $12.95   Postal Worker Exam
___ @ $12.95   Sanitation Worker Exam
___ @ $17.95   Treasury Enforcement Agent Exam

NATIONAL CERTIFICATION & LICENSING EXAMS

___ @ $20.00   Cosmetology Licensing Exam
___ @ $20.00   EMT-Basic Certification Exam
___ @ $20.00   Home Health Aide Certification Exam
___ @ $20.00   Nursing Assistant Certification Exam
___ @ $20.00   Paramedic Licensing Exam

CAREER STARTERS

___ @ $14.95   Administrative Assistant/Secretary
___ @ $14.00   Civil Service
___ @ $14.95   Computer Technician
___ @ $14.95   Cosmetology
___ @ $14.95   EMT
___ @ $14.95   Firefighter
___ @ $14.95   Health Care
___ @ $14.95   Law Enforcement
___ @ $14.95   Paralegal
___ @ $14.95   Real Estate
___ @ $14.95   Retailing
___ @ $14.95   Teacher

To Order, Call TOLL-FREE: 1-888-551-JOBS, Dept. A040

Or, mail this order form with your check or money order* to:

LearningExpress, Dept. A040, 20 Academy Street, Norwalk, CT 0685

Please allow at least 2-4 weeks for delivery. Prices subject to change without notice

*NY, CT, & MD residents add appropriate sales

L E A R N i N G E x p R E S S

An Affiliate Company of Random House, Inc.